Advance Praise for *Playing the Long Game*

"This book is jam-packed with useful information and examples relevant for coaches, parents, and athletes. At its heart, it offers tips for listening to and 'reading' your athlete. And in my opinion, this skill is foundational for helping athletes reach their goals in sport and life. I highly recommend you read it and use it as a guide if you are in the role of supporting athletes."
—*Scott Yates, National High School Hall of Fame Football Coach*

"As I have sat with numerous elite-level athletes over the last 15 years in my practice of clinical sport psychology, I have often craved a 'how-to' book for parents of highly motivated and talented performers. Ms. Breeze and Dr. Schimmel have filled a huge gap in the available information for parents of high-level athletes. It is a great resource for parents who want to improve, not only their ability to better support their child, but also, perhaps more importantly, their overall relationship with their children."
—*Tom Golightly, Ph.D., Psychologist and Assistant Director of Athletics Counseling, Brigham Young University*

"An exceptional psychological resource for parents of elite and collegiate athletes about how to show up.... And I couldn't imagine it coming from more respected professionals in the field who have decades of experience in this space! Excited to see how this improves the games for everyone involved!"
—*Jessica Bartley PsyD, MSSW Senior Director, Psychological Services, U.S. Olympic & Paralympic Committee, and Clinical Associate Professor, Sport & Performance Psychology, University of Denver (This view is my own, not that of the USOPC or any of its members or affiliates; the view may not reflect their views.)*

"As a coach, I've seen firsthand the powerful impact these conversation strategies have had on parents, athletes, and team culture. Sue and Maureen have worked with my team for years. The athletes whose parents participated in their program show up better equipped to handle the athletic and academic challenges throughout the year. I highly recommend this book to all coaches, parents, and athletes who want to improve."
–Jamie Franks, Head Men's Soccer Coach, University of Denver

"This book is essential reading for any parent of an elite athlete. It's the first book that put words to my experiences and gave me concrete processes to approach even the most difficult situations. It's packed with evidence-based strategies and supporting research, yet easy to read. I wish I'd had this sooner on my journey parenting DI and DIII athletes."
–Dr. Lisa L. Billings, Adolescent and Young Adult Clinical Psychologist

"Parents of athletes – How would you like to help your athlete navigate challenging conversations and manage their relationships with coaches and teammates? Nothing is more important than helping your child take charge of their athletic experience. Learn the helpful language it takes to create a space for listening and perspective seeking. This is an unbelievable resource that you didn't even know you needed! It's a must-read!"
–Lynn Coutts, Deputy Athletic Director for Student Athlete Excellence, University of Denver, and Mike Coutts, Head Softball Coach, Colorado School of Mines

"*Playing the Long Game* is a great resource for parents of serious athletes. It offers guidance to parents in navigating the challenging issues that arise as their children participate in college athletics. The book provides strategies for empowering children—helping to support them as they solve their own problems. I would encourage every parent and every high school and college coach to study Maureen Breeze and Dr. Sue Schimmel's approach."
–Wendy Brandes, Lawyer, Adjunct Professor, and Parent of Two College Athletes

"I have been coaching at the collegiate level for over a decade and have seen the whole spectrum of parental engagement. This reader-friendly book helps parents prepare for and navigate conversations that can change parent/child relationships for the better. For parents, it's not about changing the child but about shifting the way they show up that can make the biggest impact. Even when parents have great relationships with their athletes, *Playing the Long Game* can only make them better."
—*Logan Davis, Head Wrestling Coach, Southern Virginia University*

"As a collegiate coach for over 30+ years, I've seen the tremendous investment and sacrifice parents of high-level athletes make. I've also seen how challenging the college transition can be as athletes and parents renegotiate their relationship from separate places. The information in this book reminds us to be reflective and thoughtful in support of our children's goals in a way that builds confidence, resilience, and accountability. I love the practical applications and real-life scenarios backed by science and research. This resource will help parents navigate this new stage in their athlete's development. It will be invaluable for the parents of my athletes."
—*Melissa Kutcher, Head Women's Gymnastics Coach, University of Denver*

Playing the Long Game

A HANDBOOK FOR PARENTING
ELITE AND COLLEGE ATHLETES

Playing the Long Game

A HANDBOOK FOR PARENTING ELITE AND COLLEGE ATHLETES

Maureen Breeze

Suzanne Schimmel, Ph.D.

*To the many athletes, coaches, parents, and
readers who have contributed to this work, thank you.*

Maureen and Sue

Playing the Long Game: A Handbook for Parenting Elite and College Athletes
by Maureen Breeze and Suzanne Schimmel

Published by The Coach Athlete Parent Project

www.coachathleteparentproject.com

Cover and book design by Blue Linen Creative, Inc.

ISBN: 9798840710722

CONTENTS

Why Read This Book?

Have you ever wondered how you can help your child cope with the unique challenges of elite athletics?

Have you struggled to have good conversations with your child about athletic performance?

Have you ever thought about calling a coach to express dissatisfaction with your athlete's experience?

Have there been times when you didn't know the right thing to say when your athlete experienced a significant setback?

If you said "yes" to any of these questions, this book is for you.

If you are parenting an elite athlete, you probably are familiar with walking the fine line between support and interference in your child's athletic career. You may be wondering if you are doing the right things, or if there is more—or less—that you could be doing to contribute to your child's development and success in athletics and other areas of life. This book offers insights and strategies to help you better understand your elite athlete's unique experiences, challenges, and needs, and to guide you in being the best support system you can be.

The content is based on the latest behavioral science research from sports psychology, business, and our combined professional experience working with sports teams and elite athletes. Stories, tools, and practical tips are integrated throughout the book to help you effectively apply the strategies presented.

As parents of college athletes ourselves, we understand the dedication it takes to support an elite athlete's journey and the emotional pressures parents experience. Over the years, there were times we wrestled with what to say to our athletes in the face of disappointment and wondered whether to offer a hug or a gentle nudge. We hope the research, insights, and anecdotes shared here will assist you on this journey.

The tools offered in this book are designed to help you support your athlete and to nurture a positive, healthy, lifelong relationship.

We invite you to explore additional resources at our website: www.coachathleteparentproject.com.

All the best,

Maureen and Sue

How You Can Help Your Athlete Show Up for Optimal Performance

Parenting an elite athlete is a big commitment. Competing at the highest levels demands time, energy, and sacrifice from both athletes and their parents. Athletes are expected to prioritize training and competing above all else in their lives. At the same time, parents are often expected to drive countless hours, travel for competitions, and manage costly training fees.

When children play at recreational levels, parents may be integrally involved in coaching and supporting their children as they learn the sport. They may enjoy attending practices and watching every competitive event. Every player on the team gets an end-of-season trophy for effort, and the emphasis is on fun as well as on skill-building and competition.

When an athlete transitions from recreational play to elite levels of competition, everything changes, including the role that parents play in their children's lives.[1,2]

At the club and elite levels, coaches usually expect parents to take a back seat and to support the vision and mission of the program from the sidelines and at home. Once an athlete launches a collegiate career, coaches want to deal directly with athletes, not with parents. This transition can be difficult for parents who have dedicated many years to managing and supporting their athletes' development, and who, in the best of ways, genuinely share their child's dreams.

The complex part of this transition is that athletes still need their parents for critical support when they progress to high levels of competition. In fact, a parent's influence directly impacts an athlete's well-being and ability to thrive as a top performer.

The importance of positive parental support was recently demonstrated by NCAA-funded research on the role of parental involvement in the success of college athletes.[3] This study revealed that athletes whose parents were involved in their lives in positive ways had lower rates of depression, drug use, alcohol abuse, and risky sexual behavior. Athletes whose parents were over-involved or under-involved did not fare as well. The NCAA concluded that positive parental support was one of the best contributors to an athlete's well-being and success.

The important message in this research is that the goal isn't for parents to become less involved as their children age but to transform how they are involved.

What does positive parental involvement look like? Experts agree that it includes knowing how to be caring and present, without engaging too much or too little. Many believe it is the most important work parents can do for their athlete's overall development in their late teens and early adulthood.[4, 5, 6, 7, 8]

For most parents, the long game is to raise an emotionally healthy and productive son or daughter and to sustain a strong, positive relationship. An integral part of this journey involves helping a child learn to become independent so they can feel confident making decisions, speaking on their own behalf, and feeling motivated to live a satisfying life.

Supporting a child on this journey to autonomy can be filled with trials and tribulations, particularly in the face of the unique demands placed on parents and athletes in the complicated world of elite athletics. The unusual expectations of high-level competition may delay the journey toward independence for these athletes. In some sports, parents may need to be involved in their athletes' daily lives in ways that inadvertently slow down the development of autonomy. Athletes competing at elite levels also have less unstructured time to spend with their peers, which may impact their social-emotional development.

Some elite athletes may leave home at a young age to live in specialized housing to train and compete at the highest levels. These athletes must learn to manage their own daily lives and to achieve functional independence. However, they may miss out on important developmental stages with their parents and peers who ultimately foster emotional growth.

Fortunately, the work parents do now to support their athletes on the road toward independence will take root more quickly and effectively than at later times in life. The human brain develops rapidly from adolescence into young adulthood, at a rate second only to the rate of growth in children from birth to five years old.[9] Children will more easily pick up the life skills promoted in this book during this significant period of development. The lasting benefit is that the skills and internal resources that contribute to the success of elite athletes also create the foundation for a productive and satisfying adult life.

A critical component in the role of parents at this stage is to transition from doing something for or with their child to supporting their child to do it independently.

The importance of parents making this shift was highlighted in a study that measured stress levels in mothers and their school-aged children while the children worked on challenging digital puzzles.[10] Mothers were instructed to sit next to their child and offer words of support and encouragement but not advice. As the puzzles became more challenging, the physical markers of stress in mothers and children increased. When the mothers became uncomfortable watching their children struggle and started giving advice, their own stress levels decreased. Giving advice made the mothers feel better. Surprisingly, however, the children's stress markers increased when they got advice from their mothers! A mother's advice, even if well-intentioned, contributed to her child's stress. Support and encouragement did not.

The transition to sideline support can feel uncomfortable and unnatural for parents, especially during the adolescent and young adult years when the stakes are high. It can be difficult to withhold advice, and instead offer support and encouragement, even when parents understand that athletes benefit by discovering solutions and solving problems independently.

Yet, the study of mothers and children suggests that parental advice can interfere with an athlete's performance and with the parent-athlete relationship. Athletes are significantly more likely to be resilient and self-motivated, and better able to tolerate stress, when they get the right kind of support from parents and coaches.[11, 12]

What do college athletes have to say?

In our work with Division I athletes, we were interested in learning more about the relationship between athletes and their parents. We conducted online surveys of approximately 50 athletes about their parents' involvement. Below are some responses that illustrate the impact of different types of parental involvement on athletes' experiences.

What do you wish your parents knew about your life as a college athlete?

- How much their support means to me and how helpful it is that they are proud of me whether we win or lose.

- It is important for me to fight my own fight and speak for myself.

- Some aspects of the recruiting process and playing a college sport make me question my self-worth.

- It is much more demanding than anything I've done before. It requires attention to detail, focus, and hard work, every single day.

- Parents won't understand the coaches' decisions and what goes on with the team completely, and that's okay. Parents should be there to support you, but not to be involved in what goes on.

- Yelling and being mad at me for my mistakes isn't going to make me any better.

- I don't want them to know anything since I am intentionally trying to separate family life and soccer life.

- It has been worth all the time and money.

What do your parents do that is helpful to you as an athlete?

- One thing they do that is helpful is not stepping in. They just let me do what I need to and learn for myself. Another helpful thing is not urging me to come home and understanding when I want to stay on campus and train.

- They have continued to call me and have spent hours on the phone with me when I have been going through difficult times in school, on or off the field.

- They encourage me and let me have my own space to handle my own situations.

- They have gone to games and showed me their support and love, which can help keep me going when things get really tough.

- They helped me come to terms with my body image due to being muscular and bigger because of how strong I need to be to play.

- They are always there to vent to as an outsider, and they give me space.

- My parents have made sure that my sport is not my entire identity.

- They have helped me by letting me handle all of my sport-related stuff. It is my thing so why do they need to get involved with the coaches? Another thing that has been helpful is that they have come to most games. It is nice talking through the game with them even though they do not know a whole lot about my sport, they just give fresh eyes.

What do your parents do that is not helpful to you as an athlete?

- Wanting to talk on the phone at inconvenient times and not really asking how school is going, which I would like if they did every now and then.

- One thing that has not been helpful for me is that my parents think I can do no wrong and I am perfect in their eyes. Sometimes honesty is better in those situations. They coddle me a bit.

- My parents have been amazing, but sometimes they need to just listen when I tell them things and not act. Sometimes I am just thinking out loud or venting, and that doesn't require them to do anything after.

- They compare me to other people or to teammates.

- When they try to get too involved, it can hurt the student athlete. They need to keep an open mind that their son will not start every game and won't play amazing every day. We are trying to develop ourselves, and sometimes we have to do that on our own and deal with things ourselves.

- My dad struggles to talk to me about anything other than my sport. It seems like that was what our relationship was built upon.

How could your parents better support you as a collegiate athlete?

- Help me when I ask, but stay reserved when I want to deal with something myself.

- Keep reminding me to see my sport in the greater context of life.

- Support my mental health and try to understand through listening about the toll a sport can take on an athlete.

- I think they have done a great job. I don't have anything else I would ask from them.

- I need time before I talk about games or results. I am someone who wants to talk through those things, but sometimes I want to wait a bit to talk about them so I can individually process how I feel first.

- I would like to have my parents stay completely out of my sports life. I would rather them not come to any of the games anymore.

- They can just keep trusting that I am doing the right things, and I hope they understand that I will constantly be in good hands no matter what.

- Try to understand that I am not perfect.

These responses reflect a range of experiences and underscore the difficulty of finding the right balance for parental involvement. While many athletes were happy with the ways their parents showed up for them, others described a need for more space and autonomy. Each athlete is an individual with a unique personality and history.

Still, there are strategies that every parent can use to find the right balance and support their athlete successfully. Our mission is to share practical, evidence-based tools that will help you to be an effective source of comfort and wisdom for your athlete as they navigate the increasing demands of elite and collegiate sports.

Playing the Long Game is organized around 9 Pillars of Success for athletes.

PILLAR 1: Show Up Ready to Learn and Grow

PILLAR 2: Show Up Focused on What You Can Control

PILLAR 3: Show Up Prepared to Be Proactive and Resourceful

PILLAR 4: Show Up Ready to Communicate and Manage Your Relationships

PILLAR 5: Show Up with a Professional Mindset

PILLAR 6: Show Up with Emotional Awareness and Flexibility

PILLAR 7: Show Up Resilient in the Face of Failure and Setbacks

PILLAR 8: Show Up Ready to Receive and Process Feedback

PILLAR 9: Show Up for Your Team

Each chapter explains why the Pillar of Success is important, what factors commonly get in the way, and how parents can best support their children in developing the skills needed to show up and be successful. Each chapter also offers strategies for new ways of talking with your child and other tools to help guide you along this journey. The final chapter discusses how you can show up as a parent to create a lasting, positive impact in your athlete's life.

In each chapter, look for:

- STRATEGIES IN ACTION: These are sample dialogues that illustrate how our conversation strategies might play out between a parent and an athlete.

- CONVERSATION QUESTIONS: These are conversation starters you can use to initiate a constructive discussion with your athlete.

- QUESTIONS FOR YOUR REFLECTION: These offer opportunities for you to reflect and apply the concepts to your personal experience.

What are conversation strategies?

Athletes thrive when they have a parent's receptive ear. Knowing how to listen and facilitate your athlete's self-reflection and decision-making process can be one of the greatest gifts you can give. Productive conversations are not always easy, especially when your own emotions get triggered. You have most likely invested heavily in your athlete's success and deeply feel their disappointments. And yet, if you can create room for your athlete to experience and manage difficult situations without having to worry about your reactions, it will help them develop the clarity and strength to grow and persevere.

Our conversation strategies are based on research and used in executive and business coaching to foster exceptional leadership and high-performing teams. Our methods also closely align with Motivational Interviewing (MI), originally pioneered in the medical field. They involve strategies to foster self-awareness around goals and the internal motivation to achieve them.

These conversation strategies encourage you to ask questions that place choice and control over decisions squarely in the lap of your athlete. The process makes it clear that you are on their side while also shifting responsibility for change and growth fully onto your athlete. Learning to have a conversation in this way will have the added benefit of supporting your child in life beyond athletics.

Look for these highlights throughout the book:

- WHAT TO LISTEN FOR: For each Pillar, we share tips on how to listen when you are talking with your athlete. Paying attention to your athlete's choice of words and tone of voice can tell you a lot about his attitude toward a situation. Does he say I have to, or I should rather than I get to when discussing an upcoming game? Is his tone heavy, frantic, or enthusiastic? You can also listen for patterns. Are there times in the season when your athlete is more likely to be stressed, lash out, or lose focus?

- WHAT TO ASK: Thought-provoking, open-ended questions will help your child clarify her thinking, inspire a vision of what's possible, shift perspectives, and galvanize action. It's easy to fall into the advice trap when talking to your child. Parental advice can be helpful and necessary, but it is often more important at this age and stage of development for you to facilitate your child's thinking process, help her learn to manage problems, and generate solutions on her own. You can begin to transfer the ownership of a challenge from you to your athlete by utilizing the open-ended questions listed in each of the following chapters.

- WHAT TO ACKNOWLEDGE: When people feel heard and seen, it reduces their emotional upset.[13] Acknowledgement statements— referred to in the psychology world as empathetic statements— are great emotion metabolizers. You can acknowledge how your athlete is feeling without validating everything he says about an experience. For example, your athlete might call you to express frustration that he lost his starting position, and he feels he has been unfairly robbed of his role. You can acknowledge and empathize by saying, "I can see you are really frustrated and angry" without validating his perception (or misperception) that he was treated unfairly.

- WHAT TO SPOTLIGHT: Spotlighting is a tool you can use to help your athlete acknowledge her successes and effort. When spotlighting a current success, you can go beyond a simple congratulations or nice job and shine light on the effort and actions that contributed to the success. When she is navigating challenges, you can help her create pathways and energy for overcoming obstacles by spotlighting strategies that have worked in the past.

- WHAT TO CHALLENGE: There are times it is helpful to challenge your athlete, not to judge or shame, but to help him see where there are incongruencies in his thinking. For example, he might say his goal is to make the top traveling team for his club, but he rarely signs up for additional coaching when available. A short statement to open a dialogue might be, "You've talked a lot about wanting to advance to the top team, yet you don't seem interested in taking advantage of these extra training opportunities. I'm curious what that's about." Throughout the book, you will read about ways to help your child recognize these situations and also to constructively challenge his thinking when he's held back by limiting beliefs or a lack of awareness.

You may be thinking "all this sounds great, but my child hardly talks and rarely shares his experiences with me." If that's the case, don't be disheartened. This is not uncommon. Developing open lines for deeper communication can take time. Try consistently using the strategies discussed in this book, such as asking questions instead of giving advice, and you may well see your athlete start to open up in new ways.

A Few Important Notes

Before you get started, we have some comments to make about the way we have written this book.

We intend for the principles discussed to apply to all athletes, whether competing in individual sports, such as skiing, tennis, or gymnastics, or in team sports, like lacrosse, football, or volleyball. You will see examples from both individual and team sports used to illustrate our points throughout the book.

Second, the target audience for this book is any adult raising an athlete competing at an elite level. For ease of communication, we refer to parents throughout the book. However, we recognize that non-parental guardians, grandparents, aunts, uncles, other relatives, and/or family friends may also play a significant role in an athlete's family structure. We are confident that the lessons shared will be helpful for any adult in close relationship with a young athlete.

Third, the guidance offered in this book is targeted toward athletes in high school and college who are between the ages of about 16 and 25 years. We recognize that this is a broad age range that encompasses different developmental stages. There will be variation in the pace at which individuals move through these stages. Individual differences in life history and experience also have a critical influence on development.

We believe that the strategies offered can be applied to any individual at any point in this age range, and we trust parents to know their children and adjust their support appropriately. For ease of communication, we refer to your child or your athlete throughout the book, recognizing that high school and college-age students usually no longer identify as children per se.

We also intend for our strategies to apply to individuals of all genders. We have tried to make our language and this book as inclusive as possible by switching pronouns (he/she/they) by chapter.

Finally, we acknowledge that most of the research and experience cited in this book are based on American sports culture. There is tremendous variability and cultural diversity among athletes competing at elite performance levels. Our goal is to apply the latest findings in the research that impact athletic performance and parent-athlete relationships in most families.

Questions for Your Reflection

What do you value about the experience of parenting an elite athlete?

_____

_____

What are you most concerned about when it comes to your child and sports?

_____

_____

What role do you see yourself playing in your athlete's journey?

_____

_____

How would you describe your relationship to your child in the context of athletics?

_____

_____

PILLAR 1

Show Up Ready to Learn and Grow

One of the most important qualities athletes can bring to their sport is the willingness and capacity to learn and grow. Yet, there often is an inherent conflict in showing up every day prepared to evolve as an elite athlete.

To learn and grow requires taking risks. It demands that athletes push beyond what's familiar to try something new, whether it's changing their alignment while swinging a golf club, trying out a new position on the field, or experimenting with a different pregame warm-up. Learning and growing means making mistakes, failing, asking for help, and integrating feedback, all of which can feel very uncomfortable. It might even mean surrendering being the best today to become the best tomorrow.

At the same time, most elite athletes are expected to perform at high levels consistently. When so much emphasis is placed on performance outcomes, it can be daunting for an athlete to hold on to a mindset that allows for improvement and to take the risks required for growth.

Behavioral scientists have been studying the factors that influence a person's capacity to learn and grow for many years. Dr. Carol Dweck's research on growth vs. fixed mindsets helps explain this process.[1] Coaches and athletes have successfully applied her insights for nearly two decades, and we will use her framework to guide you in supporting your athlete's ability to harness his potential.

Growth vs. Fixed Mindsets

Dr. Dweck's work centers on two beliefs that impact an athlete's ability to learn, grow, and improve. Simply put, a growth mindset is the belief that you can improve your abilities with effort. In contrast, a fixed mindset is the perception that your talent and abilities are innate—once you reach a certain level, you can no longer improve your performance.

You might not see yourself or your high-achieving athlete as having a fixed mindset. But how often do you make statements to yourself like, "I'm not creative," "I'm not good at math," or "I'm not good at sales?" Or, perhaps you've heard your athlete say, "I'm not flexible," or "I'm not good at sprints," or "I'm not an outside shooter." Such statements may signal a belief that ability is a fixed trait that can't be improved. Unfortunately, fixed mindset thinking can negatively impact an athlete's ability to show up ready to learn and grow.

The coaches of the Blackburn Rovers, a soccer team from the UK Premier League, consulted Dr. Dweck because many of the most talented players from the training academy were not reaching their full potential. This situation was no surprise to Dweck. She is used to seeing a fixed mindset in naturally talented players who have excelled for years without being challenged. If an athlete is consistently praised for exceptional talent early in his career but then one day begins to struggle, he may believe that he has reached his limits and is no longer exceptional. With his identity as a great athlete at stake, it is hard to suddenly develop the humility to dig in and grind rather than rely on his natural athleticism or physical gifts. Facing developmental adversity and plateaus can be tough for an athlete. A growth mindset is critical if an athlete is to fully reach his potential.

Dweck's research provides insights into differences in the way people with growth vs. fixed mindsets respond in situations relevant to athletic performance.

SITUATION	FIXED MINDSET	GROWTH MINDSET
Facing a Challenge	Avoids Challenges	Embraces Challenges
Confronting an Obstacle	Gives Up or Gets Defensive	Persists in the Face of Setbacks

Applying Effort	Sees Effort as Useless	Sees Effort as the Path to Mastery
Handling Criticism	Ignores Useful or Negative Feedback	Learns from Criticism
Dealing with Others' Success	Feels Threatened by Others' Success	Finds Lessons or Inspiration in Others' Success

One of Dweck's most important lessons is that mindsets are fluid. You can have a fixed mindset in one moment and shift to a growth mindset in the next. Or, you might have a fixed mindset in some areas in your life and a growth orientation in other areas. Conscious shifts in mindset are not always easy. It takes reflection, perseverance, and risk to shift from a fixed to a growth mindset in a positive way.

Before we explore strategies to help your athlete develop a growth mindset, we will examine some of the obstacles that prevent this way of thinking.

What gets in the way?

Performance can be impacted by the way an athlete thinks about his ability to face challenges. When athletes experience failure or get negative feedback, they may focus on the criticism and form limiting beliefs about themselves. In the psychology world, such beliefs are often referred to as cognitive distortions, which are exaggerated or inaccurate thoughts that can negatively impact one's self-image and motivation. Cognitive distortions often reflect negative self-talk.

Most of us have experienced self-limiting thinking at some point in our lives. For example, have you ever received a performance review where you've been told about many things you do well and one thing you can do to improve? After leaving the meeting, the only thing you can remember is the single "area of improvement." It seems to cloud your perception of the overall performance review. If you've had an experience like this, most likely you have experienced cognitive distortion.

Self-limiting thinking and cognitive distortions come in many forms. The book *Feeling Good* describes the common cognitive distortions listed here.[2]

As you read through this list, reflect on which apply to your athlete and how this way of thinking impacts him. Consider, too, how these distortions might affect you and your interactions with your athlete.

ALL-OR-NOTHING THINKING: Sees things in black and white categories; struggles to see both the positive and negative qualities in a person or situation.

OVERGENERALIZING: Sees a single negative event as a never-ending pattern of defeat; transfers feelings about a negative event or situation into other areas.

MENTAL FILTER: Looks for evidence to support their negative beliefs.

DISQUALIFYING THE POSITIVE: Rejects positive experiences or compliments by insisting that they "don't count" for some reason; maintains a negative belief that is contradicted by everyday experiences.

JUMPING TO CONCLUSIONS/MIND READING: Interprets events negatively before considering all the evidence or when the evidence doesn't support a person's conclusion; comes to a conclusion based on how someone is behaving without having other supporting evidence.

THE FORTUNE TELLER ERROR/PREDICTING THE FUTURE: Anticipates things will turn out badly and feels convinced that his prediction is an already established fact.

CATASTROPHIZING: Focuses on the worst possible outcomes of a situation; believes the worst outcomes will happen even if they are highly improbable.

EMOTIONAL REASONING: Assumes that his negative emotions reflect the way things really are: "I feel it; therefore it must be true"; makes an intellectual determination based on how he feels.

SHOULD STATEMENTS: Motivates himself with "shoulds," "should nots," "musts," and "oughts"; relies on external expectations, shame or guilt to motivate action.

PERSONALIZING: Sees oneself as the cause of some negative external event for which he was not primarily responsible.

These cognitive distortions are common! It's easy to imagine a baseball player making an error on the field and then spending hours worrying that he will lose his starting spot (catastrophizing). Or, a lacrosse player, sidelined the previous season with a serious knee injury, panicking after tweaking his shoulder in practice, fearing that it will lead to another serious injury (overgeneralizing). Distorted thinking like this can impact an athlete's ability to accurately assess a situation, identify where he has control, and effectively apply effort for growth and improvement. In a nutshell, cognitive distortions contribute to a fixed mindset.

The good news is that negative thinking patterns can be transformed by recognizing and calling attention to them when they occur. You can help your athlete become aware of his distorted beliefs. You also can pay attention to how your athlete assesses new situations and opportunities. Many people will categorize new situations as threats if they feel unprepared or don't think they can rise to the challenge. If your athlete sees competition as a threat, his fear responses will be triggered, and his performance may suffer. But if he sees a new situation as a challenge to tackle—and he feels equipped to rise to the occasion—he will be more likely to perform at his best and be resilient even when things do not go well.

People assess competitive situations differently. There may be times when you are sure that your athlete is ready to face competition, but he does not assess the situation in the same way. Statements such as, "Don't worry, you've got this!" are well-intended but can fail to address your athlete's own experience. While a statement like this can boost one athlete's confidence, it can leave another feeling misunderstood. Using the conversation strategies presented in this book can help you support your athlete as he thinks about and works through challenging situations.

How can you help your athlete?

As we mentioned in the opening chapter, your role as a parent is changing. When your athlete transitions into elite or collegiate competition, your role shifts from "doing/thinking/planning for him" to supporting through dialogue. As you build a pattern of thoughtful conversations with your athlete, be mindful of what you are hearing, what you are saying, and the questions you are asking.

To start, let's look at a few simple strategies to support a growth mindset. Begin by listening to what your athlete says. Do you hear him use the word *never* a lot? "I will never be a starter" or "I will never be a defender." Does he often say *can't*? "I can't beat that time" or "I can't score from the left." Maybe he makes statements like "I am not a closing relay runner" or "I can't hit the curve." There is great power in these kinds of declarations.

Negative thinking can strangle growth and development. As a parent, you can challenge statements that fuel a fixed mindset.

Carol Dweck suggests that you can help shift your athlete's thinking by interjecting the word **yet**–I can't beat that time, yet, or I am not a closing relay runner, yet. This simple, three-letter word creates an arc of time for improvement and transforms permanence to possibility. If your athlete learns to incorporate the word yet into his thinking, he'll be positioned to shift into a growth mindset.

A second strategy is to ask questions that help your athlete determine what he can control and how he can apply effort to improve in those areas. For example, your athlete expresses frustration after being sidelined for weeks with an injury. He's losing ground physically and concerned he may lose his starting spot. After acknowledging his frustration, you might ask him what is within his control while he is sidelined. You can help him explore opportunities by asking questions such as:

- What can you do to improve your learning of the game during this time?

- What can you do to improve your leadership on the team while being sidelined?

- How might you use these three weeks to improve the way you show up as an athlete?

You'll read more about structuring conversations around these kinds of questions in a later chapter.

A third strategy is to remind your athlete to regularly ask himself, "What can I learn from this situation?" When he experiences defeat, critical feedback, an injury, or other obstacles that interfere with his performance, using this simple refrain–*What can I learn?*–is very useful. This powerful question immediately shifts the perspective to a growth mindset where new information and insights can impact future outcomes.

How do you know if your athlete is viewing performance situations as a threat or as a welcome challenge? Listen to how he talks about the upcoming situation. Is he feeling ready and excited? Does he think he has the necessary skills? Or, does he seem to be feeling overwhelmed, outmatched, or out of control? If you sense the latter, ask questions that help him to be curious about what might be contributing to these feelings. You can ask when he remembers feeling confident and prepared in the past and how those times compare to the present.

Or, ask if there are things within his control that he can focus on during the competition instead of focusing on what he can't control.

The same holds true for distorted beliefs. Using open-ended questions to help your athlete be curious about why he interprets a situation the way he does can uncover the concerns and fears that might be contributing to distorted thinking.

Curiosity is a powerful tool for cultivating a growth mindset. Being curious as a parent can help you pause instead of jumping in with advice and creates time and opportunity for your athlete to think and reflect. When you model curiosity, you help your athlete think differently about his mindset and the assumptions he is making that ultimately may interfere with his performance.

Strategies in Action

Below is our first example of a hypothetical conversation between parent and athlete. We know that these sample conversations might sound too good to be true. This kind of dialogue may be a long way from a typical conversation you usually have with your child. Your athlete may not be as open to discussion as the one in this scenario. You might find that you can only ask one or two questions before the discussion ends. That is all right. It is a start.

It might feel awkward and uncomfortable to shift the conversation dynamic from direct advice or emotional reactions to open-ended questions. It may take time to integrate these strategies into your conversations. We assure you that it will get easier with practice. Eventually, you'll find your own style and cadence for facilitating important reflective conversations.

The purpose of these scenarios is to offer guideposts for dialogues that can create room for reflection. They will show you how open-ended questions can facilitate deeper thinking, ownership, and better rapport between you and your child. So even if your conversations at home don't feel as "clean" as these examples, at least not at first, that is all right.

For this first dialogue, imagine your son calls to say he just failed the pre-season fitness test for his lacrosse team. You know this test is grueling and that the coach challenges players to be fit and ready at the start of the season. Your athlete, who is new to the team, has an opportunity to retake the test next week, but he is worried that his initial failure will cost him a place on the team.

SON: I can't pass the fitness test. I'm going to lose my spot.

PARENT: How many more times are you allowed to take the test?

SON: Two, but really, this is so hard.

PARENT: So you haven't passed the fitness test, yet.

SON: My time is way off. I'm worried I can't pass the test at all.

PARENT: If you take the test again next week, how might you prepare for it?

SON: I prepared for the test today. I've been running every day this past month. I haven't been sitting around.

PARENT: I have seen you running, and I know you put in a lot of effort to get in shape. How did the players who did pass prepare?

SON: I don't know. The ones who passed are seniors, and they've done this before. I guess I could ask them.

PARENT: So you think they might have strategies that help?

SON: Probably. It seemed like they had it figured out, and it wasn't that hard for them.

PARENT: It sounds like they might have some good suggestions. What else might you do to train differently this week?

SON: Well, it was the sprints at the end that killed me. I felt pretty good at the start with the long run and drill tests.

PARENT: How can you prepare for the sprints this time knowing they were the hardest part for you?

SON: Maybe I could run the sprints at the beginning and end of each of my workouts, so I am doubling up on them this week.

PARENT: Doesn't sound like a bad idea. How was your energy throughout the test?

SON: I've been focused on staying hydrated so that wasn't a problem. The strength and conditioning coach has been talking to us about sleep and diet a lot already. Maybe he'd have suggestions for what I should do this week. I was worried about cramping, so maybe I didn't eat enough.

PARENT: So do you believe that you could improve your time—even just a little—by making some tweaks with your strategy, training, and food intake?

SON: Yeah, I don't know if I can improve it enough, but I do think I could take a little off my time.

PARENT: That sounds like you'll be taking steps in the right direction.

The goal of the conversation is to help him think through the problem and come up with a solution that is within his control. If he owns the plan, he will be more likely to follow through and fully commit to it. You are helping him develop valuable problem-solving skills.

Once he successfully passes the fitness test, you might ask, "What were the most important things you learned from this experience?" Then, be open to listening to his insights. This final step reinforces the thinking and actions that led to his success so he can more fully appreciate that he was able to handle the situation. It also helps him reflect on how he responded to an overwhelming or seemingly impossible situation.

Again, it is important to ask open-ended questions from a place of curiosity and genuine interest in knowing how your child is thinking. If he senses judgment or that you have a "right" answer in mind, he may be less likely to recognize his own insights and take full responsibility for what is within his control.

To close this chapter, here is a story about Michael Jordan that Dweck relays in her book *Mindset: The New Psychology of Success*. Many of you may know that Michael Jordan was cut from his high school varsity basketball team. What you might not know is how his mother reacted. She didn't placate him. She didn't make excuses or place the blame on the coaches. Instead she told him that if basketball was important to him, he needed to bring discipline to his life. He needed to do the work. In her own masterful way, she challenged him to adopt a growth orientation, and he listened. He started leaving the house every morning at 6:00 a.m. to practice before school. Ultimately, it was his commitment to practice and work that shaped his career. Jordan's coach at the University of North Carolina said that his athletic talent alone wasn't responsible for the team's NCAA success. His work ethic set a standard for the team and elevated everyone's performance.

Conversation Questions

To wrap up, we offer these questions for you to ask your athlete when the types of situations described in this Pillar arise.

- *What can you learn from this difficult situation?*

- *What is the opportunity here?*

- *Who might you become as a result of navigating this challenge?*

- *What have you learned about yourself from past challenges that you could apply here?*

- *What are three possible rewards you could experience by pushing through this difficulty?*

- *What are you willing to commit to for your growth?*

- *Are you willing to be uncomfortable in order to grow?*

Questions for Your Reflection

What is your personal relationship to sports, and how does that impact your perspective on your child's experiences?

_____

_____

Where does your child typically fall on the fixed-growth mindset spectrum? Where do you typically fall? When does your athlete find it difficult to have a growth mindset?

_____

_____

Which, if any, of the cognitive distortions show up in your child's thinking? Which, if any, show up in your thinking as it relates to your child's athletics or abilities?

_____

_____

What strategies have you used in the past when your child resists taking on a healthy challenge?

_____

_____

Show Up Focused on What You Can Control

Athletes need to master the ability to focus and concentrate on many elements, like technical development, endurance, and mindset. As Hope Solo, World Cup champion and goalkeeper for the United States Women's National Soccer team from 2000 to 2016, once said, "Athletes are extremists. In training, it's laser-like focus."[1] However, laser-like focus on the wrong things can quickly derail athletic performance. An athlete must learn to intentionally and effectively focus on what is within her control. She cannot control a referee's bad call, but she can control her response to it. She cannot control her coach's decision to move her out of the starting lineup, but she can control her approach to subsequent training.

When we think we have no control in a difficult situation, we are more likely to surrender and feel helpless.[2] Conversely, we are more likely to persevere when we perceive that something is within our control. When an elite athlete learns to focus her attention on what is critical in the moment and on what she can control, she can develop a solid growth mindset and be positioned for high-level performance.

Dr. Carol Dweck's work on growth mindset revealed the power of acknowledging individual effort over outcome in a given situation. In her early experiments, Dweck worked with cohorts of preschool-aged children who were given a series of puzzles that grew in complexity. One cohort was praised for their success. The feedback emphasized how smart and skilled each child was at doing puzzles. As the puzzles became increasingly difficult, however, these children often stopped trying. Failing at more difficult tasks challenged their perception that they were smart and skilled, and stifled their motivation to continue.

With the second cohort, Dweck focused her feedback on the children's effort. Instead of saying, "Great job solving this puzzle," she would say, "You really worked hard. Great concentration." The praise was related to the effort, not the outcome. Interestingly, this cohort continued to work on the puzzles even when they became more difficult. When lauded for focus and tenacity, these preschoolers rolled up their sleeves and welcomed the challenge.

The bottom line? If you want to position your athlete to welcome challenges and embrace difficulty, praise her effort. The effort she puts forth is typically something within her control. This strategy is consistent with coaches who remind athletes in big competitions that if they leave it all out there, they can feel good about their performance regardless of the outcome.

Adopting a Process Orientation

There is an important distinction in this Pillar between outcome-oriented goals and process-oriented goals. Outcome-oriented goals are results that may include factors outside of an individual's control, like a starting spot on the roster, an undefeated season, or a championship trophy. These are great aspirations for any athlete. Yet, no individual athlete can control all of the factors required to win the championship or finish a season undefeated.

In contrast, process goals are based on taking steps that an athlete can control. Process goals help athletes manage focus and clarify actions that will keep them moving in their desired direction.[3] Setting process-oriented goals is one of the most important tools your athlete can use to keep focused on what is within her control.

Let's look at a specific example. Consider a soccer striker who sets the goal of scoring ten times in the upcoming season. She is setting an outcome-oriented goal that involves factors outside of her control. This player may be unable to meet this goal if, for example, she does not get the playing time she expects throughout the season. If scoring is her only goal, she may not have other tangible markers to chart her growth and improvement.

Alternatively, this player could set three process-oriented goals that she can control that also will ultimately position her to be a leading scorer. She might commit to spending three additional hours a week shooting with her left foot, practicing her take-off at the beginning of a sprint to improve her speed, and receiving short passes on the left side of the field from her midfielder. By adopting process goals that are within her control, she will be able to grow and develop regardless of her playing time—and also improve her chances of scoring when she's in the game.

There are many reasons a process orientation is beneficial in goal setting. Having a plan with manageable, identifiable steps along the way helps an athlete stay engaged and on track even when progress is slow or plateaus. In addition, process goals decrease burnout. They highlight small wins and can energize and motivate a player. Even if an athlete fails to achieve her desired outcome, she can still feel a sense of pride and accomplishment in her effort and successes along the way.

Dealing With Performance Anxiety

Performance anxiety is common among elite athletes. The high stakes and uncertainty around outcomes at the elite level create conditions in which athletes often feel anxious about their performance. Additionally, self-pressure or perceived pressure from teammates, coaches, family, and/ or the community can contribute to anxiousness.

Athletes definitely benefit from some nervous energy. It helps them get pumped up and ready to perform. However, excessive nervous energy can interfere with clear thinking, attention, emotions, and physical performance.[4] Focusing on what is within an athlete's control is a good tool for decreasing performance anxiety.

So how do you know when the pressure is too great and adversely impacting your child? For some athletes, it's obvious. For others, they may simply report that they don't feel like themselves when they cross this threshold. You can listen to hear if your athlete expresses any of these common signs of performance anxiety.

- COGNITIVE: Trouble focusing on playing and staying present in the moment; difficulty making effective decisions during competition;

struggling with memory retrieval and learning new plays, strategies, and tactics.

- ATTENTION: A narrow focus on what might go or has gone wrong rather than a broader focus on the field, court, or the competitive event; distraction; missed communication and cues from teammates and coaches; limited perception of what is happening in the moment.

- EMOTION: Increased irritability; fear or aggression; out-of-control feelings; experiences of feeling shut-down and disengaged; self-critical and feelings of worthlessness.

- PHYSICAL: Tunnel vision which causes athletes to lose peripheral vision; dry mouth due to changes in saliva; increased heart rate; tightness in chest; increased muscle tension; increased blood pressure; gastrointestinal distress. All of these changes can lead to tiredness despite being in excellent condition. This might feel like heaviness in the legs, less stamina, and shortness of breath.

Your athlete may not always be able to control the onset of anxiety, but she can focus on controlling her response to it. There are many personal strategies available to control anxiety, such as practicing conscious breathing, engaging in mindfulness moments, directing her attention to helpful thoughts or cues, and repeating a personal statement or words that reset her attention. These methods can help shift her attention and reset her thinking after an unnerving mistake, bad play, or poor referee call. By turning specific behavioral responses into habits, athletes can rapidly reengage and refocus after high-stress moments and avoid anxious mental spirals that negatively impact performance.

If your athlete experiences anxiety symptoms that interfere with her performance on a sustained basis, consult a psychologist trained to work with athletes for additional support.

What gets in the way?

Does your athlete sometimes have trouble staying focused on what is within her control? If so, she may be wrestling with a tendency toward perfectionism, a need for immediate results, and/or underdeveloped self-awareness. Each of these mindsets can impact her outlook and her performance.

Many athletes focused on outcome-oriented goals tend to define themselves primarily by external measures. This way of thinking can reflect a perfectionist mindset, which leads to unrealistic standards. Expectations for a flawless performance conflict with learning and growing from mistakes. Individuals with a perfectionist mindset often struggle when they reach plateaus. And athletes who feel pressure to be perfect, whether it's real or imagined, are more likely to experience depression, anxiety, and burnout.[5]

Few parents intend for their child to feel that their love and respect are conditional upon athletic performance. However, an athlete may misinterpret a parent's zeal for her success as a condition of love, and teens are more likely to tend toward perfectionism when they believe their parents' approval is tied to their performance or competency. Fortunately, a parent's focus on growth and development, along with unconditional support, can help combat perfectionist tendencies.[6]

In contrast to perfectionism, striving for excellence—defined as having great quality and value—can be healthy when it encourages your athlete to take risks and to learn from her mistakes. Remember, however, that excellence is not a fixed or absolute state. The pursuit of excellence is a journey in which self-esteem is linked to the process more than to the outcome. Humans are hardwired for learning. And thinking about excellence as a process sets your athlete up for learning in a positive way. In fact, when we learn something new, we often receive a surge of the feel-good hormone, dopamine, that reinforces the learning process.[7]

There is a fine line between a healthy striving for excellence and unhealthy perfectionist tendencies that plague many athletes. When your athlete is in the mode of striving for excellence, she is moving toward targets she has defined as being within her control. And when you talk honestly with your athlete about how she perceives excellence and how she is thinking about her personal improvement, you will help her shift from fear-driven perfectionism to desire-driven growth.

Expecting or needing immediate results is another mindset that can inhibit an athlete's ability to show up focused on what she can control. We live in a time with nearly instantaneous access to information. In fact, the phones in our hands provide more computer power than NASA had in 1969 when it landed the first astronauts on the moon.[8] Generation Z (born after 1996) has been raised with this technology giving them the capacity to get an answer to almost any question with a quick Google or YouTube search. As a result, Gen Z has been denied many experiences that reinforce the ability to tolerate the discomfort required for mastering challenging skills and maintaining focus over long periods of time.

Process-oriented goals help cultivate patience by providing tangible, small wins that encourage the athlete as she works on developing excellence. You can help your athlete understand that progress can be slow at times, and that learning to keep focused, even when things feel frustrating, is invaluable athletically, academically, and professionally.

Finally, underdeveloped self-awareness is a third element that can impact an athlete's ability to show up focused on what is in her control. An athlete requires a strong internal compass to decipher what is within and outside of her control. By asking your child the simple question, "What is within your control here?" you can help her think more clearly about herself and her development, and hone her internal compass. This process can be difficult for many people. The American theologian Reinhold Niebuhr captured the essence of this challenge in his well-known serenity prayer, "...grant me the serenity to accept what I cannot change, the courage to change what I can, and the wisdom to know the difference."

Developing this wisdom can be particularly difficult for athletes feeling pressure to perform well from themselves, their teammates, peers, coaches, and even a fanbase. Today, many elite athletes are managing a social media presence that is directly tied to their performance. Creating an online persona or brand and fielding both criticism and praise can be a costly distraction, and also entangle your child in arenas where she has little control. Managing her reactions to other people's disappointments, and knowing how to separate herself from these experiences, are critical for an athlete's emotional and physical well-being.

As parents, you can ask powerful questions such as:

- What is helpful for you to remember as you manage your social media?

- What are the costs and benefits of engaging with social media at this point in your life?

- What possible boundaries might you establish so that social media doesn't distract you or impact your performance?

Additional questions will be introduced in the next section to help your athlete reflect on what's within her control and to focus precious energy on the things that will help her grow and develop.

How can you help your athlete?

When talking to your athlete about focusing on what is within her control and sticking to process-oriented goals, we suggest using a What/How/Who framework to guide her reflection.

First, focus on **what** she hopes to achieve when setting a goal. Knowing what is to be accomplished and having a vision of what success looks like is critical for setting the direction and harnessing the energy to tackle the challenge. Yet, if your athlete has her eyes on a prize without a clear plan for achieving it, it is highly likely that the goal may never become a reality.

Second, focus on **how** your athlete can engage in the process of creating a solid, process-oriented action plan in response to her goals. Third, keep in mind **who** your athlete is and who she needs to be to achieve her goals. What part of herself does she have to pull forth to be successful in the moment? Does she need to be bold? Or humble? Does she need to be more curious, assertive, demanding, or patient? Does she need to dig deep and show some grit, above all else?

Learning to engage different personality traits appropriately for any given situation can be a valuable skill for young adults to develop as they prepare to navigate a variety of complex challenges in their lives. The simple process of calling attention to and naming specific qualities needed for success can help athletes be mindful of who they need to be to rise to the challenge when success doesn't come immediately.

Imagine your daughter was an All-American field hockey player who started every game in high school and led her club team in scoring. She's now committed to playing with a top Division I collegiate team, and you suspect she'll start at the bottom of the roster in her freshman year. A constructive conversation with her about who she needs to be in this next chapter of her athletic career may help her to shift her mindset. If she decides that being humble and patient are her top priorities during this time, for example, she may be better positioned to make the adjustment to a new team and new coaching styles. This kind of shift in mindset can help her better manage her role on the bench and remind her to learn all she can in practice as she waits for her opportunity to shine in the games.

Another way to support your athlete with this Pillar is to acknowledge her effort. As parents, we often praise our child's successes—the wins, the good grades, the mastered skills, and other achievements. It is easy to fall into the trap of focusing too much on our athletes' accomplishments. Remember that you will be more effective at helping your athlete develop a process orientation if you focus on calling attention to and praising her efforts. As discussed earlier in this chapter, Dr. Carol Dweck's studies show that acknowledging effort instead of outcome can encourage an athlete to develop perseverance, embrace challenges, and accept difficulty as part of the growth process. It is particularly important to take this approach when your athlete is working toward a stretch goal that most likely will involve a series of failures before an eventual success.

As you talk with your child about her athletic and academic endeavors, be mindful of the way you frame your questions. Focus on the experience and process rather than on outcome or performance. For example, a question like "What grade did you get on your history test?" focuses on the academic outcome. Questions like "What are you learning in history class?" or "What is interesting about the books you are reading for history?" keep the focus on the process of learning. If you want to check in about athletics, you can focus on the process by asking, "How did your body feel this week?" or "How is it working with the new trainer?" instead of "Will you start this week?" or "How many points did you score in the scrimmage?"

As a high-performing athlete, your child faces constant assessment and competition. She will appreciate your focus on her experience rather than on her performance.

On a final note, it can be powerful to reflect on the areas where you have the most control in supporting your child. The questions below might help you think about how you can position yourself to be an effective source of support for your athlete.

- Where do I have control in this situation?
- Where do I want to keep my focus?
- What goals do I have for my relationship with my child beyond athletics?

Strategies in Action

In these examples of parent/athlete conversations, look for how the parent uses questions to further the conversation and create opportunities for the athlete to solve her problems instead of giving advice or telling the athlete what to do. Notice how these conversations unfold in ways that keep the focus on the athlete instead of on the parent.

In this scenario, imagine your daughter calls home while she is away at a highly competitive tournament. Her squad lost a game to a team that had heavily recruited her last season. She says that she played poorly and that her less-than-stellar performance cost the team the game. "The girls on the other team talked smack to me the entire game. I think their coach told them to get into my head," she says.

Your daughter will be playing against this team in the tournament finals. You can tell that she is focused on her opponent's behavior and how it impacted her mental game, and she is stressed about the next game. This is an opportunity to help her explore what is within her control. She cannot control the other players or coach, but she can control her own responses to their taunts.

PARENT: What happens when they talk smack to you?

DAUGHTER: I get irritated. I get angry.

PARENT: That's a natural response. What happens to you then?

DAUGHTER: I miss the play. I'm slower to the ball. I get pissed at them.

PARENT: It sounds like you're saying they distract you. They pull your focus.

DAUGHTER: It totally pulls my focus. Especially because I know they are doing it on purpose.

PARENT: What might you do to quickly regain focus when you get distracted?

DAUGHTER: I don't know. Maybe take a deep breath.

PARENT: What else?

DAUGHTER: I could also say to myself, be present. Coach talks about being present in our bodies. She also talks about maintaining our position on the field. So maybe I could focus on my field position.

PARENT: Which one of these could you experiment with this weekend?

DAUGHTER: Probably just telling myself to take a deep breath. That would help me focus on myself and not on that person.

PARENT: That's a good point. Have you ever tried this?

DAUGHTER: No.

PARENT: Do you want to practice it now?

DAUGHTER: Sure.

PARENT: Okay. Close your eyes. Imagine you are in a game and your opponent starts taunting you. Take a deep breath. Now refocus on something in your body. Something like feeling your feet on the ground or relaxing your shoulders. Now, what does that feel like to you?

DAUGHTER: It feels like I've got control. Like she's not stealing my focus.

PARENT: That's good.

DAUGHTER: It feels quiet, and like I am not going to be "set off" by this person.

PARENT: It sounds like it will help you be unfazed.

DAUGHTER: Yeah, confident and unfazed.

PARENT: Perhaps you can try this approach and see how it works. You can always refine it and try different approaches. Figuring out how to tune out distractions like this is a discovery process.

By naming the impact of the problem—in this case distraction—your daughter can more easily create a plan for maintaining focus. Putting words to feelings or internal experiences helps to turn down the emotional dial and creates room for problem-solving and learning. She can then create a plan to fight this type of distraction, and this ultimately will be less of an energy drain than fighting a human competitor trying to sabotage her game. Of course, while this example features an athlete distracted by smack talk, others may thrive on such talk and use it as fuel for performance. Again, each athlete is different.

As with any important conversation, it is critical that you find the right time to talk with your athlete. Initiating a deeper level conversation when she is not receptive has the potential to backfire. Try to determine if the timing is right for her to engage in a conversation with you by being curious and asking open-ended questions. You may also notice that these types of conversations do not happen all at once. You might get to ask only a few questions before the conversation moves on to a different topic. You can always revisit it at a later time. In addition, some athletes may simply prefer to handle situations on their own without talking to a parent. This kind of autonomy is a normal part of maturation.

We close this chapter with a story about Olympic gold medalist and two-time World Cup champion, Megan Rapinoe. After a strong start to her college career, Rapinoe tore her left ACL. She spent months on the sidelines and in rehab. She returned to play, but after only two games she tore the same ACL a second time.

Rapinoe shared that experiencing these injuries ultimately helped her develop patience. "There are some things you can control and some you can't," she said. "Be patient. Focus on what you can control. There's no rushing your body, so don't put yourself on a timeline. Be patient with the healing and be kind to your body...it tests you. But I think it helped me grow and learn how to take care of my body."[9]

"I know this sounds weird, but getting hurt was one of the best things that ever happened to me. It really gave me a different perspective...I would never wish it on anyone, but I don't wish I could take it back."[10] Rapinoe concluded that her injuries taught her patience and about the limits of control, and they helped her realize how much she loved the sport and wanted to make it her career.

Conversation Questions

To wrap up, we offer these questions for you to ask your athlete when the types of situations described in this Pillar arise.

- *What is your goal in this situation?*

- *What is within/outside of your control?*

- *What is critical to focus on in this situation and what behaviors will help you achieve this goal?*

- *What obstacles do you anticipate?*

- *What is motivating you right now?*

- *Who do you need to be to achieve this goal?*

- *What do you have the power to do today?*

Questions for Your Reflection

When does your child struggle with situations outside of her control? How do you respond when she feels helpless?

_____

_____

How might you differentiate excellence versus perfection in the context of your athlete's efforts?

_____

_____

How patient is your athlete when it comes to working toward long-term growth and results?

_____

_____

How do external pressures impact your child (social media, societal expectations, family expectations, etc.)? How do external pressures impact you (scholarships, the pressure to show up at games, pressures to donate to the team/club/university, volunteering)?

_____

_____

Show Up Prepared to Be Proactive and Resourceful

If you are the parent of an elite athlete, chances are you have heard coaches talk about the pleasure of working with athletes who are highly coachable. In this chapter, we focus on two important qualities inherent in being considered coachable: being proactive and being resourceful.

Proactive athletes anticipate, take initiative, and manage situations before they become problematic. Resourceful athletes know how to take advantage of available opportunities and play an active role in managing their own athletic development. They are creative problem-solvers and can be depended upon to get things done. Athletes who are proactive and resourceful are well-positioned to fully partner with their coaches and teammates to pursue their highest potential. In this chapter, we hone in on how you can help your athlete develop this capacity to be proactive and resourceful both on and off the playing field.

SPOT OPPORTUNITIES AND ANTICIPATE PROBLEMS: Athletes who learn to spot opportunities and anticipate problems are better positioned to succeed; these skills are particularly valuable in team play, where positioning is a critical part of the game. An athlete who can read the field and look several steps ahead knows how to be in the right place at the right time for scoring opportunities.

These skills are also important when it comes to managing relationships. Being able to spot potential problems or opportunities and initiate critical conversations with coaches and teammates, before problems erupt or opportunities pass them by, is an invaluable asset. We will discuss this in greater depth in Pillar 4: Show Up Ready to Communicate and Manage Your Relationships.

These abilities can help athletes proactively manage themselves as well. Decisions regarding nutrition, hydration, rest, and time management, can all be improved when an athlete looks ahead and makes proactive choices to improve their chances for success.

RESIST PASSIVITY: The sooner an athlete learns to take initiative and resist letting problems fester and grow, the better off they will be at managing their own athletic development. Imagine your athlete learns that a position they would love to play will be open in the next season. If they do nothing except hope that they will be considered for the role, their chances of being selected will be far lower than if they take proactive steps to prepare for the opportunity, such as initiating a conversation with the coach, asking what specific skills they can work on in the next three months, and using that feedback to adjust their training regimen.

Well-intentioned parents can get in the way of an athlete's initiative and inadvertently foster passivity. When an eager parent assumes the responsibility of thinking, instigating conversations, and making plans for the athlete, the athlete can easily slip into the passenger's seat. If this happens regularly over time, the athlete might never learn how to drive their own process. Instead of jumping in with advice or instructions when you see an opportunity or a potential problem, try asking your child a few open-ended questions such as:

- What might be the opportunity here?

- What would an ideal outcome in this situation look like?

- If you were able to take care of this potential problem before it escalates, what steps would you take?

- What do you think would be the best thing to do here?

By asking such questions, you can help your athlete think about what is possible and how they might take action.

ENGAGE IN PROBLEM-SOLVING: Being proactive requires both the willingness to take action and the ability to solve problems. A parent of a starting Pac-12 football player relayed a great example of this attribute. In one of the player's classes, the professor delayed the date of an exam in order to give students more time to study. Unfortunately, the new test date fell on a day when the student-athlete was committed to traveling with his team for a game. Earlier in the semester, this professor had said she would not give special accommodations to athletes, and the player suspected that she had a bias against football players. Nevertheless, he decided to take initiative, and he spoke to her immediately after class to address the conflict. He did not wait for her to offer solutions to handle the problem because he suspected she would think he was looking for a way out of the test. Instead, he proposed sitting for the exam on the original test date. By communicating, owning the problem, and presenting a possible solution, he proactively handled the problem while also managing any potential negative bias about athletes.

IDENTIFY RESOURCES: Knowing how to think creatively about problems and identify potential resources helps athletes succeed in athletics and in life. Think about a person you know who always manages to get the job done. Often, this person is not the smartest or most skilled, but, rather, the most resourceful. Resourceful people know whom to call for help, where to find information, and how to leverage what is at their fingertips.

Resourceful people typically have high levels of practical intelligence. Practical intelligence includes a capacity to think quickly on one's feet, navigate one's surroundings, implement ideas, adapt, and possess "street smarts." These are skills that can help an athlete on and off the field. Dr. Robert Sternberg, a renowned psychologist who studies the impact of different types of intelligence, finds that practical intelligence can be as important as analytical and creative intelligence in achieving high levels of success.[1]

Generation X (born between 1963 and 1980) are characterized as the most resourceful generation.[2] Many of this generation had working parents and grew up as "latchkey kids." They often navigated their daily lives with a lot of independence. If they wanted to do something, they were typically left to their own devices to figure out how to make it happen. This generation ordinarily managed large amounts of unstructured time and independence during childhood, and were allowed to do things like ride their bikes around the neighborhood without supervision. They babysat or delivered newspapers to earn spending money. These experiences contributed to the resourcefulness that marks this generation.

Many young people growing up today have had more highly structured and highly supervised childhoods than Gen Xers, and they have not had the same opportunities to develop resourcefulness and independence. We will talk about ways you can help your athlete be more resourceful later in the chapter. For now, reflect on these questions.

- On a scale of 1 to 10, how resourceful is your athlete?
- Is your athlete willing to ask for help?
- Does your athlete identify helpful systems of support?
- Does your athlete seek mentorship for guidance?

MANAGE UNCERTAINTY: Most elite athletes face challenges of uncertainty throughout their careers. They may have to deal with wondering if they'll make a team, if an adjustment in training will aggravate an old injury, or if a new recruit will take their starting spot in the lineup. Ambiguous situations abound, and athletes who are more resourceful and proactive in managing these challenges experience better outcomes. In the professional world, the ability to handle uncertainty is a highly regarded skill, and many employers look for evidence of this ability during the hiring process.

In the previous chapter, we discussed the value of being able to focus on what is within the athlete's control. This skill is equally important in the ability to manage ambiguity. Being proactive also lies at the heart of handling the unknown. When an athlete reacts passively to an ambiguous situation, nerves and anxiety can be all-consuming. By channeling their efforts proactively in a direction where they have some control, they can better manage their energy and accomplish small goals along the way. For example, an athlete may be returning from a knee injury and might be unsure whether their knee will hold up for the season. While they can't control every element of their return to play, they can be proactive by strengthening the surrounding muscles and doing mindfulness exercises to reduce stress and shift their focus away from their injury. All of this will help them to navigate the challenging emotional experience of returning after injury.

What gets in the way?

Many preteens, teens, and young adults are overloaded in today's complex and competitive world as they juggle their classes, homework, extracurricular activities, family obligations, friends, dating, social media, and the biological need for a whole lot of sleep. In some families, teens may work part-time jobs for spending money. Or, they may be expected to contribute to the family by working and/or taking on significant household responsibilities. Elite athletes face even more extreme demands on their time with early morning training, after-school practices, and competitive events, many of which require travel and significant time commitments, added on to the already overwhelming course of daily activities. It can feel like too much for even the most well-organized athlete, and many parents naturally try to help their children with time and stress management.

Some well-intentioned parents may try to lighten the load by limiting household chores and non-sports related activities during these years. Ironically, though, it is often the low stakes experiences, like mundane household chores, jobs scooping ice cream, or mowing lawns, and casual sports experiences such as street hockey and pickup basketball, that allow teens to build the critical skills of resourcefulness and negotiation. Dealing with disgruntled customers, asking a manager for time off, and negotiating rules with friends in a pickup game, offer opportunities for athletes to practice valuable life skills. These additional responsibilities and activities can actually help athletes to be better prepared for managing the challenging demands of their athletics and academics.

We often hear collegiate athletes comment on the difficulties of being responsible for managing their lives on their own after leaving home. An athlete who is used to relying on a parent for simple things like making appointments, doing laundry, planning meals, and other daily chores, may have trouble taking on these responsibilities while also managing their academic and athletic obligations.

You may be understandably eager to make life easier for your busy child and may instinctively feel the need to intervene when adversity or challenge arises, whether in the form of a difficult relationship with a coach, a situation with a team member, or a physical plateau in development. The stakes in elite sports can be high, and families are invested emotionally and financially in their child's success. However, when parents intervene to bring about a resolution before allowing their child to try to tackle the challenge on their own, they take away the opportunity to develop critical problem-solving skills. If you act too soon on behalf of your athlete, you circumvent the opportunity for your child to sense warning signs and anticipate problems; these are skills needed for an athlete to be able to show up prepared to be proactive and resourceful.

Recognizing that too much parental intervention can interfere with an athlete's initiative and resourcefulness, how do you know when to step in, add support, and intervene? Two great questions to ask yourself are:

- What value will my intervention bring?
- What detriment might it cause?

If you are doing something for your athlete that they can both do for themself and learn from, it is best to stand back even if it costs them something in the process.

The bottom line? Give your athlete the opportunity to dig in and explore how they can solve challenging situations on their own.

It can be helpful to remember that resourcefulness is born from creative thinking, problem-solving, and dealing with a lack of easy-to-access resources. It is a muscle developed during times of need. Athletes who typically have easy access to everything they want and need may have trouble learning how to go after something that is not readily available. For younger athletes, developing this muscle could look like earning money for new gear or organizing rides to practice. For collegiate athletes, it might mean identifying and seeking out campus resources for support, setting up their own medical appointments, or asking for meetings to pursue helpful feedback.

Resisting the desire to rescue your child at the first sign of struggle could be one of the greatest gifts you can give. When parents and coaches support athletes in being resourceful and thus developing independence and autonomy, they are more likely to be self-motivated and to experience positive sport-related outcomes.[3] Failure to take ownership of a problem can interfere with an athlete's ability to be proactive and resourceful. If your child does not acknowledge problems that are theirs, they will not be inclined to take initiative and generate solutions.

Let's see how these elements played out in a real-life example. Consider a scenario in which an athlete arrived a few minutes late to practice every Wednesday. No one seemed to notice, so in the athlete's mind, it was not a big deal. However, when this athlete was nominated by their peers to be a captain for the next season, the coach pulled them aside and explained that they were not ready for the role. They had set a bad example by consistently arriving late to practice. Frustrated, the athlete claimed it was not their fault! They were late only because the professor let the class run overtime each week.

Had this athlete taken ownership of the situation and acted proactively by discussing the need to leave class at the scheduled time with the professor, while also discussing the situation with the coach, they could have managed the conflict before it escalated into a more costly problem.

How can you help your athlete?

While resisting the urge to do for your athlete what they can do for themself, you might wonder, how can I help? There are several supportive things you can do.

Listen for passive language used by your athlete. Statements such as "There's nothing I can do about it," or "It is what it is" indicate that they see the situation outside of their control, and may contribute to a passive response. You can ask questions to help them explore ways they can impact the situation like:

- If you could change one thing you are doing in this situation, what would it be?
- What would be the cost if you take no action in this situation?

Of course, there are situations in which your athlete really does lack control and must adapt or accept a situation as it is. Your wisdom and guidance in these instances can be invaluable.

You can also listen for statements in which your athlete has given away their power. For example, your athlete might say, "The coach doesn't like me. I'll never start." Or, "The seniors on the team have it out for me. I'll never fit in here." When they give all the power in the situation to the coach or the other players, they lose the opportunity to impact the situation with strategic action. You might respond with questions such as:

- What do you want the coach/seniors to know about you?
- How might you be letting these thoughts about whether the coach likes you or not impact how you show up and perform?

If your athlete acknowledges a problem on the horizon, help them think through an action plan to handle it proactively. Begin by clarifying the challenge. You can ask:

- What is at the heart of the problem?
- What needs to be addressed?
- What might happen if you ignore this and do not address it?

Your follow-up questions can help to facilitate a problem-solving process:

- If this problem worked out well, what might the situation look like?
- What resources are available to you?
- What would a first step look like?
- When would be the best time to take action?

Ultimately, you want to support your athlete in learning to anticipate potential problems and opportunities, take ownership of the situation, identify the heart of the challenge, and create an action plan. To wrap it up, you can ask your athlete how they might hold themself accountable to their goals and decisions. It is more powerful when they create an accountability plan as opposed to you managing their follow-through.

Strategies in Action

Many elite and collegiate athletes face the significant challenge of balancing a demanding academic load and athletic training. Here is an example of a student-athlete discussing this challenge with a parent. Note the arc of this conversation. See how the parent acknowledges the challenge their child is facing, asks questions to help them think through options and perspectives, and then encourages them to act.

ATHLETE: Physics is killing me. I don't know how the professor expects us to get these labs done each week, and the labs are on top of reading, problem sets, and a weekly quiz.

PARENT: It sounds like you are balancing a lot with that class and your training hours.

ATHLETE: It's impossible. There is no way I can do this.

PARENT: What options do you see?

ATHLETE: None!

PARENT: What might a conversation with the professor look like?

ATHLETE: She doesn't want to hear us complain. She said that on the first day. She's not going to change the workload. I guess I will wait until our first midterm and then take an incomplete if I fail. I've already failed two of the weekly quizzes.

PARENT: How might waiting until after the midterm create a bigger problem for you?

ATHLETE: I don't want to be a whiner.

PARENT: How could you frame a conversation that isn't about complaining, but about getting help and tips for managing the workload?

ATHLETE: She'll see it as complaining.

PARENT: Imagine you were the professor, and you had a student who was coming to class, putting in the hours to study, all while balancing a Division I sport. What would you want to hear from that athlete?

ATHLETE: Hmmm, that the athlete wasn't asking for special favors and was willing to do the work, but maybe needed some help on how to be more effective.

PARENT: So how could you approach this conversation with that in mind?

ATHLETE: Maybe tell her that I'm working hard in the course, and I believe I'm putting in the hours, but I want to do better. I could ask her if she has any strategies that could help me be more effective with learning this content. And the labs—if she had insights about how I could do a better job with the labs.

PARENT: Great. That doesn't sound like complaining. It sounds like you are making a concerted effort to get a learning routine in place before it's too late.

ATHLETE: Yes, but she has a reputation for not liking athletes.

PARENT: Well, that could be true. However, what do you want the professor to know about you?

ATHLETE: That, yes, I'm an athlete, but that I take my classes seriously. I want to do well.

PARENT: What else?

ATHLETE: That I'm not expecting her to give me special accommodations.

PARENT: It might be important that you explicitly mention this. If this meeting could go as well as possible, what would you like to walk away having accomplished?

ATHLETE: I'd like to learn tips to do better and help me study for her quizzes. I'd like her to know I'm serious about my work. And maybe find out who I might study with. I can't make the tutoring session because of training. But I'd like to find a few other people I could study with who are focused.

PARENT: So, as you prepare for office hours, what specifically can you do to get help on the quizzes and labs?

ATHLETE: I guess I could pull out my previous ones and highlight where I'm lost. That way we can make the most of the time.

PARENT: That sounds like a great idea. Knowing exactly what you would like to accomplish in the meeting will help you be prepared. So, if you wrote down three things to tackle in the meeting, what would they be?

ATHLETE: Let her know that I'm not complaining and am serious about getting help. Strategies to learn the material more effectively; and suggestions of people I might study with who are either in this section or her 9:00 class.

PARENT: So, when will you go see her?

ATHLETE: She has office hours tomorrow. If I'm there early, I can hopefully see her before training.

PARENT: That's great. Let me know how it goes.

In this situation, the parent does not offer to solve the problem nor advise the athlete what to do. The parent does, however, ask questions to help the athlete see the cost of being passive rather than proactive. The conversation gives the athlete an opportunity to take the professor's point of view and think through how a meeting could be approached in a way that does not sound like complaining. Last of all, the conversation gives the athlete an opportunity to think tactically about how to prepare for a meeting to get the most out of it—all skills that will serve this athlete throughout their life.

We close this chapter with a story of Olympic luge competitor, Shiva Keshavan. Growing up in India, Keshavan didn't have access to a training track. He didn't even have a coach in his early years. But he did have a resourceful nature. So, to practice the luge, Keshavan created a makeshift sled with wheels instead of blades and traveled down crowded mountain highways in the Himalayas. You can find videos of him soaring down roadways dodging cars and animals while practicing his technical skills. In his first five Olympic appearances, he rented or borrowed sleds. And because the Indian government does little to financially support winter Olympic athletes, Keshavan had to proactively raise funds on his own to attend competitions. Keshavan is now highly revered as a six-time Olympic competitor—both because of his athletic prowess and his determined spirit.

Conversation Questions

To wrap up, we offer these questions for you to ask your athlete when the types of situations described in this Pillar arise.

- *What are three approaches you could take to address this challenge?*

- *What are some resources that could help you?*

- *How could you benefit from addressing this challenge?*

- *Who do you know who has dealt with a similar challenge? How did they handle it? What can you learn from this approach?*

- *Imagine you are 30 years old and looking back at this time. How would you like to be able to say you handled this situation?*

Questions for Your Reflection

When do you tend to jump in with advice instead of first listening to how your child thinks about and perceives a situation?

_____

_____

How does your child respond to uncertain situations? How do you respond to uncertain situations?

_____

_____

How have your abilities to be resourceful positively impacted you in your life?

_____

_____

When are you inclined to jump in and rescue your child in situations that could help them grow and develop?

_____

_____

Show Up Ready to Communicate and Manage Your Relationships

Communicating well and managing relationships are a critical part of being proactive and resourceful. Good communication skills are particularly important in relationships between athletes and those who have authority over them, such as coaches, trainers, teachers, and professors. This skill of managing up–anticipating the needs of your superiors, taking actions that are mutually beneficial, and clarifying expectations–is highly valued in the business world and regularly discussed in publications like *Harvard Business Review* and *Forbes*. It is an important skill for athletes to develop as well.

To begin, high-performing athletes benefit by establishing clear lines of communication when managing important issues. Nagging injuries, upcoming vacations, confusion about feedback, or difficult team dynamics are all potential areas that might require proactive communication.

Imagine a collegiate athlete who is concerned about her grades and worried about her eligibility. Being proactive, she sets up a time to meet with her coach. To prepare for this meeting, she thinks carefully about how she will communicate her message by considering the following questions:

- Why is it important for the coach to know this now?

- How might my eligibility status impact the coach's plans or goals?

- What does the coach need to know about this situation and my approach to handling it?

- When would be the best time to have this conversation?

- What other information should I bring to the meeting to help the coach understand the situation?

- What can I do now to help the coach, the team, and me move through this difficulty?

An athlete who practices managing up can learn to adapt to different coaching styles more easily. However, communication may not look the same on every team or for every coach. Raising an issue with a hands-off coach will look different than doing so with a highly involved coach. It may also be helpful to consider the coach's preferences for receiving information. For example, does the coach like messages to be put in writing? Does he or she prefer meetings before or after practice? Does the coach want athletes to set up meetings a day in advance?

By considering what information needs to be shared, when it should be communicated, and how it can best be received, athletes position themselves well to manage potentially difficult situations. By managing up and providing coaches with critical information ahead of time, an athlete can avoid blindsiding her coach with potentially negative news.

What gets in the way?

Managing up requires an athlete to take ownership of her relationships with authority figures and understand that she plays a critical role in these two-sided relationships. However, there are many reasons that it might be challenging for athletes to do so.

There is a lot of individual variation in how elite athletes feel about dealing with authority figures. A child's upbringing and background can influence their comfort level with adults. For an athlete raised in an environment where it is rude to look an elder in the eye, asking a coach for an in-person meeting to raise a difficult issue can be daunting. A conversation in which an athlete needs to ask questions or share concerns with a coach can be overwhelming if she has had little prior experience talking directly to adults. These conversations can be especially challenging if a coach is not open to discussion or feedback. If this is the case, you might encourage your athlete to approach an assistant coach who seems more accessible.

It is especially important for athletes to manage relationships with medical personnel involved with their care. Often athletes minimize the role they play in the management of their own injuries. They may be hesitant to ask questions, to speak up about injuries that continue to plague them, or to discuss rehab that is not helping them make progress. Athletes may believe it is their fault if recovery isn't going well. They may be concerned that they will be perceived as weak or whiney if they speak up. Athletes who are comfortable asking questions about both their prognosis and process for care are better equipped to be partners in their health and injury recovery. It can be helpful to remind your athlete that sports medicine personnel typically welcome this kind of partnership with athletes.

Another element that can interfere with an athlete's ability to manage up is when parents get upset about a situation and intervene prematurely. If a parent initiates a conversation with an athlete's coach or other authority figure, it robs the athlete of this experience of learning how to manage up. It can be devastating to see your child lose her starting spot, get slighted on the court, receive a poor grade on her exam, or get overlooked for the potential you believe she has. It does not matter if she is 11, 16, or 21. The same alarm bells ring. It is challenging to remain objective.

However, there are times you might not have all the crucial information needed to see the larger picture. Whenever possible, it is best to look to these situations as perfect opportunities for your athlete to schedule a meeting, prepare for a discussion, and navigate a difficult conversation. Coaches respect athletes who self-advocate, and in fact, many expect them to do so. It is important to make sure you are not inadvertently short-changing your athlete's personal development by stepping over her and taking charge of a situation yourself. In addition, some coaches get frustrated by parental intervention and can unconsciously take out this frustration on an athlete.

By stepping back and allowing your child to take charge, you also avoid triangulation. Triangulation happens when three people are involved in a conversation but are not talking directly with each other at the same time. Miscommunication often occurs in these indirect conversations, and difficult situations can become exacerbated.

If your athlete is talking with a coach and the situation is not progressing as quickly as you would like, you might pause and consider the following to help you put the brakes on your instincts to jump in and take over the situation.

First, think about your own motivations. How do they align with your athlete's goals? Second, ask your athlete whether she wants you to be directly involved. We often hear coaches share that they field conversations, phone messages, and emails from parents about an athlete's playing time, position, scholarships, and the like. To make things more difficult, parents regularly ask coaches not to share their inquiries with the athlete. This puts coaches in a difficult position and adds an additional layer of challenge to what may already be a hard situation for your child. So, if you do decide you must go forward with taking action, include your athlete in all your communications so that you can move forward together.

Of course, safety along with mental and physical health concerns are issues coaches want and need to hear about. There may well be times when you need to step-in and manage a difficult situation. Playing time, team dynamics, and athletic improvement issues are best handled by the athlete. But suspected physical, sexual, or emotional abuse and safety concerns definitely warrant a different kind of parent involvement.

If you have a concern about your child's safety or welfare, identify the appropriate person in the athletic department or club organization. You can also seek the support of a mental health, medical, or safety professional in your community. Other resources that may help are SafeSport and the sports administrator or Title IX coordinator (for collegiate athletes).

How can you help your athlete?

While your restraint allows your athlete the opportunity to develop the skills for managing critical relationships, you can still support her by raising helpful points for her to consider. One of the most powerful things you can do is to help your athlete understand the perspective of the coach, professor, or other authority figure.

Start by asking her to reflect on the following questions to broaden her point of view. You might also consider reflecting on these questions yourself to gain greater insight into your athlete's experience.

- If you were the coach, what would you expect?
- What might the coach want to see from you? Why might this be important to the coach?
- What else might the coach be thinking about in this situation?
- What might the coach need to know about your experience to fully understand the situation?
- If you were the coach, what information would you want to know and have conveyed in this situation?

You can follow up with the questions below to continue to raise your athlete's self-awareness.

- What do you expect you will hear and why?
- How do you feel about the coach (this person)?
- How might these feelings impact what you say and do?
- In a year from now, what would you like to be able to say about how you handled this challenge?

One note: if your athlete is not inclined to reflect verbally, she may be more open to doing so in a journal. The act of journaling helps to organize thoughts, put words to feelings, and reduce anxiety.[1] When practiced regularly, the process builds self-awareness and helps to track "self-talk," goals, and insights.

You can also help your athlete understand how to effectively listen to the other person when navigating a difficult conversation. If she can adopt a mindset of listening to learn—rather than a mindset of trying to win an argument or make her case—she will build greater rapport and possibly gain invaluable insights. One of the best tools to stay in this mindset of listening to learn is to engage curiosity.

How might she stay curious about what is being said? Encourage her to ask herself questions such as:

- Why might my coach have this viewpoint?
- What might be behind this way of looking at things?
- What might be blocking my coach's understanding of my point of view?

And of course, remind your athlete to ask questions when she is confused or concerned about something said in a conversation with an authority figure. You might also invite your athlete to role-play a conversation with you if she is open to it. Nothing helps more than practice and real-time feedback.

When facing a conversation that is rife with conflict, Aldo Civico, former director at the Center for International Conflict Resolution at Columbia University, suggests shifting from a problem-based approach to an opportunity-based approach.[2] To experiment with his strategy, call to mind a conflict you've recently experienced.

Now think about the following questions:

- What was the problem?
- What caused it?
- What was blocking a solution?
- Who was at fault? Who was to blame?
- What limitations did you face in dealing with it?

Take a moment to reflect on how you feel. You may feel angst or anxiety, or you may feel stuck, helpless, or frustrated.

Now think about the same conflict and reflect on these questions:

- Who do you want to be as you handle this conflict?
- What inner resources will support you in accomplishing this change?
- How might this change impact your life?
- How will you look and sound?

- How might you feel differently by approaching the conflict in this way?

How do you feel after considering these questions? If you feel lighter and more inspired, you are not alone. This second list of questions outlines a process for growth and learning. It redirects our thinking so that we can tap into deeper resources, and it frames the conflict as an opportunity instead of a problem.

Aldo Civico has facilitated conflict resolution on the international stage with this model. We have found it valuable in the sports arena as well and believe it is a powerful strategy you can share with your athlete.

Here are a few other notes to help your athlete communicate well. First, encourage her to engage in face-to-face interactions whenever possible. Gen Z usually prefers to text rather than call and to email rather than to meet in person.[3] When managing up, however, face-to-face meetings reduce the chances of miscommunication and limit tensions that can fester when handled via technology.

Your daughter may claim that it is faster and more efficient to communicate via technology. You can remind her that reading nonverbal cues is critical for both parties in a challenging conversation, especially when the stakes are high. Constructive resolution, not efficiency, is the goal. You might also check-in to see if your athlete may be avoiding confrontation by opting to text or email in difficult situations. It can be helpful to remind her that it is understandable to want to avoid the intensity of direct interactions. If you can help her find the courage to manage her relationships face-to-face while also helping her see that she can handle the outcomes even when they are difficult, she will learn a critical life skill with huge returns in the long run.

The same ideas apply to your conversations with your athlete. Face-to-face almost always trumps conversations via technology. However, this can be challenging if your athlete lives away from home. The NCAA's studies indicate that most parental support comes via text messages. While texting is understandable, given everyone's busy lives, texts and emails do not give athletes the same level of support as face-to-face interactions. Communication research shows that both the hormonal release of oxytocin (the neurotransmitter responsible for the good feelings we experience in close relationships), and the biological benefits received by emotionally connecting with others are largely lost when communication takes place via text or email.[4]

You'll learn more about providing support to your athlete on the neuro-biological level in Pillar 6: Show Up with Emotional Awareness and Emotional Agility. In the meantime, we encourage using FaceTime, Zoom or other technologies that allow face-to-face interactions as often as possible when your athletes are away from home.

Strategies in Action

Imagine your daughter was recruited to play shortstop at a highly competitive university. After joining the team, the coach lists her on the roster as a designated hitter and moves another player to shortstop. At first your daughter seemed okay, believing that in time she would be playing the position. However, several months into the season nothing has changed, and a series of mixed messages from the coach has her feeling confused and frustrated. She seems to be losing motivation and excitement for the team and game. Here's an example of how a parent can support an athlete from the sidelines without getting directly involved.

PARENT: It seems like you're not excited about the team right now.

DAUGHTER: I'm frustrated and don't get what the coach is doing.

PARENT: What does your coach say about it?

DAUGHTER: She tells me if I work harder and show commitment, then I will play. So, I do it and then nothing happens. The next week she says I have to show that I want it. And I think I'm doing that. I can't figure it out.

PARENT: Have you spoken directly to your coach about this?

DAUGHTER: Well, not directly. She tells us she does not want us to complain about positions and playing time. That we need to prove ourselves on the field. If I talk to her, she will think I'm acting entitled.

PARENT: From what you said before, it sounds like you are confused by the guidance you are getting. She might have a different idea of what working hard and showing commitment looks like that you are unaware of. What would a conversation around clarifying some of her directions be like?

DAUGHTER: Well, maybe she won't see me as entitled if I am genuinely asking for clarification.

PARENT: No, I don't think she will if you approach it that way. But it might be helpful to think about this situation from the coach's perspective. What do you imagine the coach is thinking about the roster?

DAUGHTER: I know she is stressed. The two injuries in the spring season left holes, and she has had to switch things around. I think she is probably wanting to show some allegiance to the seniors on the team, too.

PARENT: Those are good insights.

DAUGHTER: But I still don't see how I can have a conversation with her about this.

PARENT: How do you want to be perceived by the coach?

DAUGHTER: I want her to know how serious I am about playing shortstop. I'm not going to lie. That is the main reason why I came here. This doesn't seem fair. You were in the recruiting meetings. You heard that they were looking at me as a shortstop. She said that.

PARENT: I understand that you want to play shortstop, and you made your decision based on this assumption. But nothing is guaranteed. You are in a tough spot. I see that you are disappointed and do not blame you for being frustrated. The important thing is what you do with these feelings. The current reality is that you are a designated hitter and hoping to be the starting shortstop. And the coach seems to be juggling a lot to manage a difficult situation. So how might you address this situation in a way that is less about your disappointment, and instead, genuinely ask for help with what you can do to grow as a player on this team?

DAUGHTER: I don't know.

PARENT: What do you think would be helpful for the coach to hear from you?

DAUGHTER: That I'm not complaining, but that I'm confused. That I want to be a key contributor and want to be doing all I can on my own and during practice so that I can do this.

PARENT: Great. This will be important to explain. What else might be helpful for the coach to hear?

DAUGHTER: Maybe that I can see she's juggling a lot and probably feels pressure right now, too.

PARENT: I imagine that acknowledging the challenges she is facing will go a long way here. If you were to have a meeting with her, how could you ask for clarification around what hard work and commitment look like?

DAUGHTER: I guess I could tell her how I demonstrate hard work and commitment and ask if she looks for other things that I might be missing.

PARENT: That would be great. If you can ask for specifics, I think it would help you. And let her know that this is a learning process for you. My experience is that coaches, like bosses in the professional world, want their teams to be successful. Sometimes they don't know that their messages need further clarification. By acknowledging the challenges she is facing and really listening to what she says, I think you won't come across as complaining, but earnest and eager to do what it takes to be successful.

In this situation, the parent helps the daughter take the coach's perspective, anticipate what might happen, and strategize about how to gain clarity around expectations. If the parent simply sided with the daughter and initiated a conversation with the coach, the athlete would lose out on the opportunity to learn how to deal with authority and disappointment.

We close this Pillar by sharing a story about Zaza Pachulia, entrepreneur, philanthropist, basketball operations consultant for the NBA's Golden State Warriors, and two-time world champion basketball player. Zaza came to the United States from his native country, Georgia, when he was just 19 years old to play basketball for the Orlando Magic. Frustrated by a lack of playing time during his rookie season, he talked to his coach, the celebrated Doc Rivers, who told him, "Zaza, you just need to stay ready. I don't know when I'm going to call your name and put you in the game. All you have to do right now is be a pro and keep working and staying in shape."[5] Zaza followed Doc Rivers's advice, and, when his time came, he was ready to take the court. Zaza did the work to "stay ready." By talking to his coach, Zaza learned what he needed to be doing to position himself for success and stay on top of his technical and mental skills. When his opportunity came, he was ready and prepared to shine.

Part of an athlete's job in managing up involves understanding what a coach is looking for in terms of "staying ready." Preparing for opportunity in this way is both a mindset and active process. We suggest athletes reduce ambiguity and make sure they understand what they need to do by asking their coaches for concrete behaviors that demonstrate "staying ready." For example, does the athlete need to spend time reviewing tape, honing a particular skill, or maintaining high endurance levels? The process also involves communicating the athlete's readiness—physically, nonverbally, and emotionally—whether the coach reminds her of it or not. This "being prepared" mindset is part of the professional mindset you will read about in the next chapter.

Conversation Questions

To wrap up, we offer these questions for you to ask your athlete when the types of situations described in this Pillar arise.

- *What can you gain from having this conversation with your coach/professor/teammate?*

- *How do you believe you are perceived by your coach/professor/teammate?*

- *What might this person be thinking or feeling?*

- *If this conversation could go as well as possible, what would you hope to get out of it? How can you prepare for it?*

- *What might this person need to hear from you? What do you need to hear from this person?*

- *What are the mutual concerns here?*

Questions for Your Reflection

How comfortable is your child with having conversations with authority figures?

_____

_____

How did you get comfortable having challenging conversations? What strategies help you to communicate well and manage relationships in difficult situations?

_____

_____

How might the approach of listening to learn benefit you and your relationship with your child?

_____

_____

What makes it hard to pause and keep from intervening on your athlete's behalf?

_____

_____

Show Up With a Professional Mindset

What does it mean for a young elite athlete to show up with a professional mindset? Three key abilities contribute to a professional mindset: the ability to be consistent, to self-reflect, and to self-manage. Let's explore what it looks like for your athlete to cultivate these important attributes.

The Ability to Be Consistent

Consistently showing up focused and ready to work hard, whether an athlete feels like it or not, is at the heart of a professional mindset. Consistency in effort is essential for honing the ability to deliver results with regularity. A professional basketball player knows that the odds of consistently hitting free throws in the big game are enhanced by consistently hitting them in daily practice. It is through consistency that athletes master the skills required for peak performance.

Consistency does not mean executing perfection, but it does mean that the athlete is fully present and engaged, even when he is tired, frustrated by a loss, elated by a win, or overwhelmed by outside obligations. Of course, remaining engaged through such challenges can be difficult, and many athletes will feel the pull to give up.

One of the most effective ways for an athlete to remain consistent when experiencing resistance is to connect to his intrinsic motivation. Extrinsic motivation is easy to recognize; it is based on external rewards such as material perks, attention, money, and the approval of others. It alone is rarely enough to get an athlete through the most challenging times. On the other hand, intrinsic motivation stems from internal rewards derived from an athlete's love of his sport, the thrill of competition, or the excitement of improving his skills. Intrinsic motivation is much more powerful for athletes working through challenges.

How do athletes develop intrinsic motivation? Research shows that an individual is more likely to be intrinsically motivated when he has a strong sense of **autonomy**, feels **competent** at what he is doing, and experiences a sense of **connection** to others.[1] When adolescents positively experience these three factors, they are less likely to drop out of sports, and more likely to persevere through challenges that lead to their growth and development.[2]

Let's take a look at these three factors.

AUTONOMY: We have and will continue to highlight strategies you can use to support your athlete's journey to independence. The bottom line is that your child needs to take ownership of the actions and decisions that will advance him from the athlete he is today to the athlete he hopes to become tomorrow. His ownership is a driving factor for intrinsic motivation.

COMPETENCE: When an athlete feels incompetent, it can be very difficult to keep trying. If your athlete is struggling with a particular athlete skill and feeling incompetent, you may see his motivation lagging. But when he believes that he has some degree of competence, he will be more likely to persevere and work hard to improve.

For example, imagine your athlete excels at endurance training and loves to run, but he resists weight training. He understands that competing at the elite level requires overall strength and upper body muscle, so weight training is important to his success. However, he is not motivated to spend hours in the weight room. If he incorporates interval training that combines running with quick lifts to his training regimen, he may be able to leverage his competency and love of running to gain ground with his weight training.

CONNECTION: When an athlete relates well to others, be it coaching staff, fellow team members, or other competitors, it creates a sense of belonging that can improve overall performance in both academic and professional arenas.[3]

While a coach can create a team culture that enhances a sense of belonging, your child also can contribute to his own sense of belonging. You can help him do the following:

- Make a point of directly connecting with everyone when he arrives at training or in the locker room (verbally or physically)

- Focus on shared goals

- Be curious about others and genuinely interested in who they are

- Look for things he may have in common with his teammates and reach out to connect around shared interests

- Say "yes" to spending time together in and out of sports

- Work to accept differences

- Offer support to others in ways that show you genuinely care about them

- Ask for help when needed

A by-product of feeling connected is personal accountability. Feeling responsible to others and wanting to perform well for them contributes to an athlete's ability to move through resistance and ultimately succeed at his goals. We will talk more about accountability in Pillar 8: Show Up Ready to Receive and Process Feedback.

Another strategy that fosters intrinsic motivation is doing a "WIIFM– What's In It For Me" values clarification exercise. What does your athlete love about his sport? What value does it bring to him? What drives him to play his sport? He might care about being part of a team, traveling to tournaments, feeling like he's growing and improving, winning competitions, or being recognized in the newspaper. You can help him make a list of everything he loves about competing and help him discover the intrinsic 'whys' that balance his extrinsic reasons for playing.

Athletes are typically motivated by a balance of intrinsic and extrinsic factors. Yet, many external motivators lie outside of an athlete's control. As an athlete rises in the competitive ranks and psychological demands increase, he will benefit from having strong intrinsic motivation. By fostering his intrinsic motivation, you can help him sustain the passion to be consistent in effort.

The Ability to Self-Reflect

It is normal for younger children and even older athletes to look for their parents' reactions at games or during competition. This validation is an important part of the growth process. Yet when they reach the top competitive levels, tapping into their internal feedback loop is critical for honing skills and intuition. It gives the athlete a moment to own his experience. Additionally, if an athlete has his own insights about a situation, he will be able to have more constructive conversations with his coach and be better prepared to process the coach's feedback.

Maureen coaches dancers launching professional careers in the highly competitive ballet world. She often looks at the behavior of a dancer immediately upon exiting the stage as an indicator of a professional mindset. A dancer who looks to her for immediate feedback suggests that the dancer may still be performing for and seeking the approval of an authority figure. Maureen trains dancers to look inside themselves after a performance or competition to self-evaluate and self-review before seeking external validation or feedback.

The value of the ability to go inside, reflect, and take ownership of an experience extends beyond an athlete's performance on the field or court. Self-reflection is also important in the broader realm of owning one's choices about health, well-being, fitness, and other factors that play into elite performance and a professional mindset.

The Ability to Self-Manage

There is a wealth of research about how self-management and healthy lifestyle choices impact athletic performance and durability.[4] These choices include getting enough sleep, having excellent fitness based on exercise science, following a healthy diet for performance and recovery, and committing to good recovery routines. These self-care habits directly impact an athlete's ability to perform with consistency.

Ownership of one's lifestyle choices can be a daunting challenge for collegiate athletes who may be living independently for the first time in their lives and facing new social pressures. While some athletes need more information to make better life-style decisions, others may benefit from merely clarifying their goals and evaluating whether their choices are aligned with their athletic aspirations.

Sue works with a coach who asked athletes from a highly competitive Division I sports team to share what they wished they had known before arriving at college. Their responses reflect an awareness of the importance of making positive lifestyle choices that foster a professional mindset. We include some of these responses to highlight the types of blind spots that some athletes have when they get to the collegiate level.

I Wish I Knew...

- how to manage time better
- how important your everyday mentality is
- how to find intrinsic motivation with school
- How little self-awareness I had, and how I feared failure so much
- how important it is to have good relationships with professors
- that people will listen to me when I talk and not to be so scared to speak up
- how to take criticism and not get defensive
- to make your routines hard because they will get easier as you do them more often
- there is no time to feel sorry for yourself; if you make a mistake learn from it and move on
- how much routines impact your performance so figure out what works best for you to be ready for the day
- consistency breeds confidence, which in turn makes you even more consistent
- building relationships with teammates makes training, the locker room, travel, etc. way more enjoyable

- you can't hide, so it's up to you to leave a positive impression on coaches and teammates every day; people notice when you are only going through the motions

- how to stay confident regardless of my mistakes

- how hard it is to bring the intensity every day and not get complacent

- that just because you played as a freshman doesn't mean you'll play your sophomore year

- that managing stress is a matter of choices you make, and that you can't do everything

Many of these athletes' comments reflect the importance of making smart decisions and being prepared mentally and physically. Think back to the story in the previous chapter about Zaza Pachulia's experience as a rookie and staying ready for his big opportunity. A professional mindset prepares an athlete to be ready for critical moments. The sooner elite athletes acknowledge the importance of owning their decisions around sleep, nutrition, time management, and seeking help when needed, the better prepared they will be when they are called to a great opportunity.

What gets in the way?

One of the biggest challenges that *nonathletes* face with a professional mindset arises when they graduate from school and enter the working world. The focus in school is typically on their personal development and potential. In the working world, the focus shifts to the contributions they can make and the value they add to an organization. It can be eye-opening for young professionals to realize their bosses may care less about their growth potential and more about their day-to-day contributions.

High-performing athletes must embrace these performance expectations earlier in life. They experience tangible consequences for their daily performance and must manage these expectations daily. Athletes who adopt a professional mindset and focus on the value they bring to their team or sport will more easily adapt to these higher levels of competition.

A second challenge to honing a professional mindset involves a good old-fashioned work ethic. Elite athletes know how to work extremely hard and put forth great effort. However, some may stumble when they face internal resistance. Most athletes can attest to the internal chatter that tempts them to take a day off, choose shortcuts, or fail to give 100 percent. And when sick or injured, an athlete still must know what he can do to contribute at the highest level.

Having a consistent pre-practice routine can help to mitigate these tendencies. Preparation habits, like listening to certain music, stretching, or doing a quick meditation, can help an athlete gather mental focus and "get going." These stacked habits can reduce decision-making fatigue from battling temptations to give in or take shortcuts that can keep him from performing at his best.

There may be times when the internal resistance becomes so great that an athlete begins to question and reevaluate his relationship to his sport. It can be challenging for both athlete and parent when his relationship to his sport starts shifting, especially after years of significant physical, time, and financial commitments. Your athlete might have loved playing at first because he was the natural star of the team. Or he may have responded well to a particular style of coaching on a less competitive team. As he progresses in his athletic career, his relationship to the sport—and to his internal motivators—will evolve. It is helpful to let him know these changes are normal. You can support him in navigating these shifts by listening and asking questions that encourage him to explore and reconnect to his love for the sport.

Here are a few questions to help foster this self-reflection:

- What do you still love about the sport?
- What has changed for you?
- What would your life look like in a year if you no longer played?
- What would you miss by not playing?
- What would you gain by not playing?
- What might you regret if you quit/continue to play?
- How can I support you during this challenging time?

The challenge is to create space for your athlete to wrestle with these extremely difficult questions without inserting your own opinion. Of course, it is normal and natural for you to have an opinion, but remember that you can bring greater value to the situation by listening with your full focus and attention. Try asking questions in a neutral tone and really listening to the answers. Supporting your athlete during times of doubt and indecision is critical for his athletic growth and development. By remaining a neutral bystander, you can help him cultivate insights and develop his own opinions and relationship to the sport and these qualities will serve as fuel for his success moving forward.

If an athlete concludes that he is no longer interested in pursuing his sport, it can be a trying time for both the player and parent. We address this scenario in the book's final chapter.

How can you help your athlete?

Along with creating space for your athlete to reflect and cultivate a personal relationship to his sport, you can help him understand what it looks like to show up with a professional mindset. Talking about expectations and how to handle them will help him understand what he can do to manage his choices and behaviors.

Neuroscience confirms that decision-making is an emotionally driven process.[5] Your athlete's feelings about a situation will impact the decisions he makes. If he feels uninspired, for example, it can be harder for him to make critical decisions that advance his goals. Thus, we emphasize the importance of helping him cultivate his own reasons for playing his sport and understanding his 'why.' Your discussions together can help him to clarify why he wants to play and to reconnect with the emotional energy needed to make tough decisions.

The ability to make mature decisions requires self-awareness about one's own emotions. Psychologist Susan David from Harvard Medical School suggests that a simple 10-minute journaling exercise that connects a student to what he values and feels can protect against negative peer pressure and discourage dropping out of academic classes when they become difficult.[6] Although this research has not been tested in the athletic arena, the concepts hold promise for athletes.

Making the right choices again and again can be taxing and draining, especially when an athlete is feeling overwhelmed. Decision fatigue can result from multitasking, overindulging on digital devices, or lacking sufficient mental rest. When the brain is overloaded, it interferes with willpower and the ability to focus, making it harder to have the mental control needed to make good choices.[7]

Helping your athlete understand the importance of taking time to relax, clear his mind, and detach from technology will support him in making the right choices at critical moments to drive peak performance. Your athlete may tend to turn to gaming or social media in order to relax, but you can remind him that getting some fresh air or going for a walk are better ways of gaining energy to reset and refocus his mind and body.

Strategies in Action

Imagine your son is an elite wrestler. He has always been extremely motivated and competed at the highest levels, but recently he has been complaining about training. You know he is under a lot of academic and physical pressure, and you can tell his spark is missing. He does not seem to be his same motivated self, and you wonder what's happening.

PARENT: I'm sensing you're tired and overwhelmed. Do you want to talk about it?

SON: I don't like training lately. The coaches are on us all the time. They never cut us any slack.

PARENT: What seems different about training now compared to last year?

SON: I don't know. Last year it was hard, but we had fun. Coach always pumped us up. Now it feels like work every day. He yelled at me last week for not showing up 100 percent.

PARENT: What do you think that was about?

SON: It pissed me off. I'm never late. I never miss practice. I'm always there.

PARENT: What do you think Coach might mean by 100 percent?

SON: I know he's referring to having a lot of energy. Not just going through the motions. As a captain, I know he expects me to keep the team's energy up.

PARENT: How well do you think you have been doing that?

SON: Honestly, I'm so exhausted half the time that I'm lucky to just show up.

PARENT: You have long, demanding days.

SON: Yes.

PARENT: Do you still love to wrestle the way you used to?

SON: I don't know. I hate to admit it. I'm just so tired.

PARENT: Are there times that you feel upbeat and excited for training?

SON: I guess on Mondays. I usually feel a little better after the weekend. But during the week I run from classes, to the gym, to the library, to bed. I never have time for anything else.

PARENT: So, the weekends help you catch your breath?

SON: I think so.

PARENT: And when you are at training on Mondays feeling more rested, you like it better?

SON: I guess I do like it better on Mondays now that I think about it. I tend to feel more like myself. Coach has even commented on that.

PARENT: I know you can't go about every day like it's a Sunday, but how can you create short rests throughout your day to rejuvenate a bit?

SON: I don't know. What are you thinking of?

PARENT: I'm thinking of short periods of time—before practice or before you start your evening studying—where you can be quiet and let everything go. Maybe use a meditation app for a 10-minute meditation, listen to your favorite music, or take a walk to clear your mind. Putting routines into place that help you reenergize yourself for your next activity.

SON: I could take 15 minutes before practice every day to clear my head.

PARENT: What would that look like?

SON: I could get to the gym early before everyone else, get dressed, and go sit out by the back door in the sun. Maybe listen to my favorite music while stretching.

PARENT: What would that do for you?

SON: I think it would help me separate my thoughts. Half the time my mind is still on the test or whatever we did in my last class. I also think it would help me to be by myself.

PARENT: What if you experiment with that this week and see how you feel?

SON: I'll give it a try.

PARENT: If you don't notice an improvement, we can talk through some other choices you might make. It's natural to go through periods of being tired and perhaps a little burned out. Take note of how you feel this week and what works or doesn't work. You can always make tweaks next week depending on how things go.

In this scenario, the parent creates a safe space for the athlete to reflect on his feelings about wrestling. He is reassured that his feelings are normal, and that he has the power to experiment with changes that might energize him. At the end, the parent offers to revisit the situation in a week after he explores a few ways to rejuvenate himself throughout his day.

We end with a story about goalie Corey Crawford, a two-time Stanley Cup champion for the Chicago Blackhawks. Crawford spent five years stuck in the minor leagues while trying to keep his NHL ambitions alive. He questioned whether he had the talent to play at the top level and began to think about moving on and playing in Europe or Russia. However, he decided to stay put, focus on showing up consistently each day, and remain committed to having fun—the reason he loved to play hockey in the first place.

Crawford's commitment to reconnecting with his internal motivation for playing the sport, and to showing up in the minor leagues with a professional mindset, paid off. He has had an illustrious career with the Chicago Blackhawks, and as of 2021, he is in the top five in all-time goalie win percentage.

Conversation Questions

To wrap up, we offer these questions for you to ask your athlete when the types of situations described in this Pillar arise.

- *What does showing up as your 'best self' look like?*

- *What do you value about playing this sport?*

- *What do you believe is the best choice you can make here?*

- *What choices would your coach want the team members to be making on and off the field?*

- *How might a professional handle this situation?*

- *In five years, what do you want to say about the choices you made at this time in your life?*

- *What is getting in the way?*

Questions for Your Reflection

What life skills do you hope your child develops from his experience as an athlete?

_____

_____

How would you describe your child's relationship with his sport? How do you imagine he might describe it?

_____

_____

How do you feel when your child expresses doubt, indecision or changing ambitions in relation to his sport?

_____

_____

What intrinsically motivates you as a parent of a high-performing athlete?

_____

_____

Show Up With Emotional Awareness and Flexibility

World-class athletes understand that emotional awareness and flexibility have a significant impact on performance. Athletes were once taught that they need mental toughness, but the emphasis has shifted to mental agility. It's not about being tough and suppressing feelings, it's about recognizing that feelings are an essential part of competition and need to be channeled effectively for optimum performance in the moment.

You can remind your athlete that emotions are data. When managed well, emotions provide critical information and fuel to boost performance. Emotions do not make a person weak or strong, and do not have to be thought of as good nor bad. Rather, they can be thought of as either useful or distracting during competition and as important information for learning between competitions.

World-renowned psychologist Daniel Goleman outlines the fundamental abilities that make up emotional intelligence.[1]

- Recognize one's emotions
- Regulate one's emotions
- Use emotions to guide decision making
- Read other people's emotions
- Read social situations

Recognizing emotions involves being aware of feelings and being able to name them in the moment. This process often requires an athlete to check in with themself. It might involve developing an awareness of where in their body they are experiencing an emotional reaction. Or, it might include learning to recognize events that trigger feelings of anxiety and anger, or patterns of their own behavior that typically follow upsetting events.

The more specific your athlete can be when naming an emotion, the better. Instead of simply saying, "I'm stressed" or "I'm upset," encourage them to be more specific so that they can express, "I feel apprehensive about my wrist in practice," or "I am angry about the coach's change to our approach." Being specific when naming an emotion can help your athlete better understand what is creating discomfort. It also creates distance from the emotionally charged experience so that they can make conscious choices about how to respond. The point is not to suppress emotions but to use them effectively as information for decision-making, which is central to emotional regulation.

Athletes who demonstrate emotional agility know how to use feelings to fuel performance. Some athletes need to stoke their emotional fire to achieve optimal performance, while others need to thoughtfully regulate it. Each athlete has their own unique zone of optimal emotional intensity to perform at their best.

Emotional experiences may impact athletes differently. For example, anger might motivate one player but debilitate another. It might be helpful for your athlete to reflect on their best and worst performances. Noting the levels of stress and emotional intensity they felt at these times may help them see how their emotions either undermined or fueled their performance.

This reflective process can be particularly valuable if your athlete is working with a coach who creates levels of emotional intensity that don't align with their optimal personal level. The same can be true if they happen to have loud, boisterous teammates and prefer quiet space to gather their thoughts and focus. Simply by noting that the coach and players do certain things to fuel emotions can help your athlete take steps to manage their own emotional energy.

Not only do athletes respond to emotional intensity differently, different sports require varying levels of emotional intensity. The exactitude required for golfing typically demands more contained emotions than a sport like football that typically feeds off dynamic emotional intensity. Athletes who can effectively regulate their emotions and use them to fuel their performance have an advantage over those who easily get hijacked by emotionally charged moments.

Michael Jordan's experience illustrates this idea. Jordan was cut from his varsity basketball team and undoubtedly experienced frustration, disappointment, and probably a good dose of anger. However, he did not quit, blame the coach, punch a wall, or deflect the experience. Instead, he used his feelings as motivators to guide his decisions; he channeled his disappointment and frustration into choosing to practice on his own every morning and disciplining himself in ways that allowed his talent to flourish. Athletes who are aware of their emotions and harness them effectively to make rational choices have a competitive advantage.

Yet, we've all seen competitors who fall victim to heightened emotions and who are prone to outbursts, yelling at a referee, throwing a tennis racket, or starting a fight. Such behavior can easily derail performance. These athletes are unable to use their emotions to their advantage.

Managing emotions is a complex process involving multiple regions of the brain. Since the adolescent brain is not fully developed until the early to mid-twenties, it is common for young athletes to struggle with managing their responses when emotionally triggered.

To better understand the impact of intense emotions on performance, let's look at the science to see how athletes can use their emotional intensity to their advantage.

What gets in the way?

When an athlete experiences stress, the sympathetic nervous system activates physiological changes that protect the body from real or perceived threats by eliciting fight, flight, or freeze responses. If the level of stress is significant enough, blood and oxygen are diverted from the prefrontal cortex—the area of the brain used for decision-making and problem-solving—and channeled to other areas in the body that can physically respond to the threat. This physiological response can impair the ability to think, weigh decisions, and make choices, which leaves the individual vulnerable to impulsive actions and loss of emotional control.[2]

Of course, this response is adaptive in life-threatening situations, like encountering a bear in the woods. In a dangerous situation, your survival depends on your ability to run—not on your ability to decide whether to run. There are normally no life-or-death situations in athletics, yet the body still has the same physiological responses. A mistake in a clutch moment can trigger a physical stress response that leads to a loss of composure.

An athlete who experiences a "fight" response to a triggering event might exhibit anger, aggression, and physical outbursts. A flight response might cause so much distress that an athlete exerts a great deal of energy without focus or effectiveness. A freeze response can cause an athlete to shut down, mentally leave the moment of competition, and get lost in a whirlwind of thoughts. In this instance, you might see them with their head down, shoulders rolled forward, and a look of defeat on their face. In the heat of competition, these fight, flight, and freeze responses can lead to unnecessary fouls, game ejections, poor performance, or missed opportunities.

Athletes can benefit from the emotional intensity that increases their heart rate and helps blood flow to their muscles. The problem arises when stress becomes too great, and these fight, flight, and freeze responses are triggered at levels too high in intensity. Every athlete has their own optimal level of sympathetic nervous system activation where the stress helps them compete at their physical edge without interfering with clear thinking. This optimal level of intensity is a fine line that is easy to cross. Once crossed, there can be costly consequences. As a result, athletes benefit by having strategies to quickly recover when they become emotionally hijacked by a stress-inducing event.

How can you help your athlete?

It is beyond the scope of this book to discuss specific sports psychology strategies for athletes' emotion regulation in the heat of competition. Different athletes require different skills based on their sport and struggles.

Our goal is to help you be an effective resource when your athlete is struggling and comes to you with concerns, whether about sport or life.

The most important thing to keep in mind as a parent when supporting your athlete is to remain neutral and not get swept up in the heat of the emotions. Your emotional regulation can critically impact your athlete's. We will discuss this situation in greater detail in the next few pages and again in the final chapter, but for now, know that you can better serve your child by creating the space for them to recognize and process powerful emotions without having to worry about your emotional response.

It is helpful to remind your athlete that most everyone in the sports world has to work on managing intense emotions. Emotional upset shows that an athlete cares about winning, hates losing, doesn't like to make mistakes, and values fairness. It goes with the competitive territory. And this, too, is a process and part of the development of an elite athlete.

In his book, **Permission to Feel: Unlocking Powerful Emotions to Help Our Kids, Ourselves, and Our Society Thrive,** author Marc Brackett offers a helpful acronym that supports emotional regulation: RULER.[3] This tool underscores several elements of Goleman's attributes of emotional intelligence and can be particularly helpful when processing an upsetting event with your athlete.

R: Recognize an emotion

U: Understand the emotion

L: Label the emotion

E: Express the emotion

R: Regulate the emotion

As we've been discussing, the act of recognizing and labeling an emotion creates distance from the upsetting event and helps to turn down the intensity of what your athlete may be feeling.

Another strategy to help your athlete express an emotional experience is to ask them to rate their feelings on a scale of 1 to 10 (with 1 being mildly upset and 10 extremely triggered). Giving a number to the intensity of the experience creates awareness. Do they need to take a moment to calm down and bring a 10 to a 5 before they can thoughtfully manage the situation?

Slow belly breathing is one of the most effective ways to counter a stress-inducing event. It puts the brakes on a triggering emotion and sends an "all-safe" signal to the mind and body. Even a single breath, focusing on a deliberate and slow exhale, can begin to turn down the volume on intense feelings. This tool is especially helpful in the heat of competition when your athlete might have to process an emotionally charged event in the midst of play. However, like other skills this must be practiced to become automatic and effective.

A tremendous body of research shows that meditation increases emotional self-regulation and the ability to recognize others' emotions. LeBron James, the Seattle Seahawks, and other major athletes and teams utilize mindfulness—the practice of observing what one is sensing, feeling, and thinking in the moment—and other meditation techniques to improve their focus and ability to regulate emotions. You can find more information on breathing and mindfulness techniques on our website.

Encouraging your athlete to monitor how they feel mentally and physically throughout the day also helps with emotional regulation. When they are tired, overly distracted, and mentally fatigued, their brain is taxed so they become more likely to fall prey to impulses and emotional reactions that interfere with goals. The acronmym HALT (hungry, angry, lonely, and tired) is often used to highlight physical and emotional states that leave a person vulnerable to making poor decisions. If your child is stressed and under athletic or academic pressure, taking breaks throughout the day and being mindful of rest and recovery time will help them develop greater emotional agility. This process may feel counterintuitive to an athlete during a busy season when feeling pressed for time.

If your athlete is struggling with emotional regulation that leads to severe performance anxiety, it may be time to consider consulting professional support. Sports psychologists are trained to help athletes work through this challenging, yet very treatable condition. We suggest you consult your athlete's club, university, or community resources for a list of qualified sports psychologists.

In addition to sharing the RULER acronym and breathing and mindfulness strategies, the conversations you have with your athlete can be an impactful and lasting method of support.

As we mentioned in Pillar 4: Show Up Ready to Communicate and Manage Your Relationships, having conversations face-to-face or via video technology can help you read your athlete's nonverbal cues and better support them. The following are additional conversation notes to keep in mind.

First, simply listen to your athlete without judgment. Allow them to share their emotional experience out loud without fear of being corrected, pushed, or reprimanded. Having a safe space to voice their experience, at whatever intensity, provides an opportunity to shed some of the emotional heat they may be carrying so that they can make effective decisions for managing the situation.

On the neurobiological level, upsetting events that trigger your child can make it difficult for them to think and process helpful information in the moment. Connecting with a person who helps them feel understood often provides a calming effect in situations like this.[4] In experiencing expressions of empathy, a person feels safe. And only then are they able to think more clearly and process information to learn and grow.

The second thing you can do during these conversations is to acknowledge your athlete's experience. Acknowledgment statements let your athlete know that you see the emotional impact of what they are experiencing. You do not need to validate their perceptions of a situation, but it is helpful to validate what they are feeling at the moment. For example, if your athlete is upset because they were blamed for the relay team's loss, you can acknowledge their feelings by saying, "I get it, you're feeling blamed and angry." The acknowledgment does not have to go into whether they did in fact lose the race for the team or not. Resist the temptation to simply prop up your child. Rather, focus on letting them know you see their pain and frustration.

To get an experiential sense of this process of soothing your athlete through listening and acknowledgments before trying to engage them constructively, think about an upset baby. When an infant is crying, their central nervous system is activated. Most babies cannot soothe themselves in this state. When you respond to and pick up a crying baby, they often start to settle down because they feel safe. In effect, your central nervous system calms theirs. Once the baby settles down, you can hold them away from you, make eye contact, and engage with them. The process is similar to what you can do for your young adult athlete. Effective listening and acknowledgment statements will help your athlete feel verbally held and heard. Once they are calm, you can begin to problem-solve together.

It is easy in the competitive world of sports to think of acknowledgments and empathy as negative actions that lead to creating a soft athlete who is unable to push through adversity with grit. Some athletes respond better to empathy than to being directly challenged while others respond better to being challenged than to receiving empathy. However, based on our experiences working with elite and professional athletes, offering acknowledgment statements followed by thought-provoking questions is most effective for helping them move through difficult situations.

These through-provoking questions are central to facilitating your athlete's thinking process. At this point, it is critical to refrain from giving advice or telling your athlete what to think. It can be extremely difficult to see your child in pain. As a parent, you instinctively want to soften the blow and fix the situation. However, by asking questions and listening deeply, you give your athlete the gift of being able to sort through their experience, identify the emotions they're feeling, and create a plan for moving forward that makes sense to them. You are helping them develop a process for working through difficult situations now and in the future.

Instead of jumping in to make them feel better by saying, "Your relay team members are wrong," or "Ignore them—they just need a scapegoat," you might ask the following questions:

- How did their comments make you feel?
- What do you believe about the situation?
- What would you like your teammates to know?
- What would have been more helpful to hear from your teammates?
- If you were one of your teammates in this situation, what might you have said?

- What would you like for you and your teammates to gain from this situation?

Finally, if your athlete is prone to troubling emotional reactions, you can help them identify common triggers. Ask open-ended questions to identify patterns of what sets them off—whether it is a teammate, a coach's reaction, referee calls, or painful losses. After your athlete sees patterns in their behavior, help them identify and label the emotion they feel in these specific instances, as suggested with the RULER acronym.

The ultimate goal is for athletes to learn to identify and manage their own emotions in the moment. Going through this process with you in slow time helps to rewire their thinking and prepare for when they are engaged in their sport in real time. Learning to pause, take a deep breath, and label the emotions they are feeling buys them the split second needed to effectively respond. The more athletes practice this chain of thinking, the more emotionally flexible they'll become and more likely to stay focused to perform at their best.

Strategies in Action

Imagine your child plays basketball for an elite team and was ejected from a critical playoff game after screaming at the referee. You saw the play happen. Your athlete was flagrantly fouled, yet they were charged for the foul. You don't blame your child for getting angry but hated to see the outburst cost the team a chance for advancing to the championship. Your child has always had a fiery temper. In fact, it has made them the athlete they are today. However, you believe that if they could learn to manage it better, it would not be a liability. You decide to talk to your child the day after the game to check in.

PARENT: That was a tough call last night. How are you feeling about it today?

ATHLETE: It was a horrible call. Everyone knows it. That ref had it out for me.

PARENT: I understand you're disappointed with how it all played out.

ATHLETE: I can't believe he kicked me out of the game. Especially since I was the one who was fouled.

PARENT: You certainly were fouled. Do you think the problem was with you challenging the referee, or how you challenged the referee?

ATHLETE: I know the problem was how I did it. I shouldn't have gotten in his face. But it's my job as the captain to speak up for the team. Especially when a horrible call like that happens.

PARENT: Your fire is one of your best assets, especially when you can channel it on the court. But how do you feel when it gets out of control?

ATHLETE: Horrible. I let my team down. And I know Coach is disappointed in me.

PARENT: If you were to have the chance to replay that moment, what might have been another way to handle it?

ATHLETE: I don't know if I could have done it differently. The player could have hurt me. I was fired up. It's not like I had time to sit and think about how I wanted the scene to play out.

PARENT: No doubt it's hard to make the best choices when we're fired up. You are not alone with that. Imagine you were the ref who made a questionable call. You would expect a player to challenge you, right? But take a second to sit in his shoes. Think about what you would respond well to if you were the ref and had a player challenge you?

ATHLETE: I think I'd respond better if the player was calm, yet confident and strong. Maybe if she acknowledged that it's impossible for the refs to see everything that happens.

PARENT: What would feeling confident and strong look like?

ATHLETE: It'd be direct. I would call out what happened but in a controlled way. I know I lost it last night.

PARENT: So, what could you do when you're triggered like this to redirect yourself?

ATHLETE: I don't know.

PARENT: What if you had a mental image of you reacting in the calm, yet confident and strong way you just described.

ATHLETE: I guess if I could call that to mind immediately, it might slow me down, so I don't react so quickly.

PARENT: How might you practice this?

ATHLETE: Well, I guess I could replay the scenario from last night's game—I keep doing it anyway—but now see myself acting differently. Maybe see myself pause, collect myself, and then tell the ref what happened.

PARENT: Replaying the experience in your mind with this different outcome sounds like it could be really helpful. When you see this in your mind, what does your body do?

ATHLETE: I stand up straighter. I feel my shoulders pull back. My feet feel firmly planted on the ground.

PARENT: That's excellent. You can recall these physical sensations of feeling calm when you get triggered. How might you enlist your teammates to support you with this?

ATHLETE: I guess I could share with a few of them what I'm trying to do. If they see me get heated, they could remind me of who I want to be—confident and calm.

While it may seem unrealistic to think about how to behave in a situation ahead of time, this evidence-based strategy, known as *mental rehearsal,* can help players manage their triggers. In fact, many sports psychologists agree that the sooner athletes learn to recognize their trigger situations and plan constructive responses, the better they will be at achieving positive outcomes. Mental rehearsal, when practiced regularly, can help athletes develop emotional agility and contribute to their resilience, which we discuss in the next chapter.

We close this chapter with a story about the 1980 "Brawl in Montreal" between the infamous boxer Sugar Ray Leonard and his opponent Roberto Durán. Leonard had the speed and reach to beat Durán and was expected to win the match. However, Durán was masterful at psychological attacks, which emotionally destabilized his opponents. Before the match, Durán unleashed verbal slurs that enraged Leonard. Leonard's emotions got the best of him. He fought Durán with a fury to "beat him up" as opposed to fighting with technical skill and strategic expertise. Leonard lost by unanimous decision. His loss of emotional control had cost him the match.

Conversation Questions

To wrap up, we offer these questions for you to ask your athlete when the types of situations described in this Pillar arise.

- *What situations trigger you?*

- *What's at the core of this situation that is troubling you?*

- *What can you do to pause in the moment, collect yourself, and refocus?*

- *How can you use your frustration (anger, disappointment) as fuel for your growth and development?*

- *How can I be of help to you now?*

Questions for Your Reflection

What level of stress (and type of stress) helps your athlete perform at their best?

_____

_____

What potentially triggers your emotions in the context of your child's athletics?

_____

_____

What helps you feel calm and balanced in emotionally heightened situations that relate to your athlete? What happens when you become upset?

_____

_____

How might your emotions before, during, and after competition impact your child?

_____

_____

PILLAR 7

Show Up Resilient in the Face of Failure and Setbacks

All athletes must contend with performance mistakes, losing seasons, and threatening injuries. Developing the resilience to bounce back from failure and setbacks is a critical factor for peak performance. A resilient athlete is better equipped to stay in the game in the short term and climb in the competitive ranks over the long term.

For an elite athlete, failure can be as small as a single missed pass or as big as a lost bid for a championship. To manage a small mistake made in the moment, like a dropped ball or a fall, an athlete must move on immediately. At the highest levels of competition, he must be able to immediately reset and reposition. Dwelling on a mistake can cost him dearly. Resilience and emotional agility are a must.

Resilient athletes can recover from mistakes, learn from setbacks, and maintain passion even when progress is slow. They know when and how to ask for help. They are not afraid to take risks.

Showing up resilient in the face of failure and setbacks is a quality that also helps athletes throughout life. The time your athlete spends honing this prized trait will pay off in a variety of arenas. In her work as an executive coach, Maureen finds that resilience is a highly sought-after professional skill. A senior executive once shared that the number one thing he looks for when hiring is a track record of resilience. It is no surprise that business leaders seek to hire former athletes.

To build resilience, an athlete must experience adversity. Think about building muscle and physical strength. A muscle must be pushed and stressed with resistance or weight. An athlete's resilience is groomed in the same fashion.

While some people are naturally more resilient than others, this skill can also be taught. Parents can foster resilience in their children.[1] Helping your athlete process failure is a first step toward building resilience.

Psychologist Dr. Martin Seligman spent years studying the impact of failure.[2] He found greater resilience in people who can see failure as temporary, local, and changeable. What does this mean exactly?

Temporary means viewing a failure, whether it is a lost game or a losing season, as limited within a scope of time. Just because his team failed this year doesn't mean his team will always fail. The acronym FAIL (first attempt in learning) is a great way to keep a temporary perspective of failure in mind.

Local means containing the failure so that it's not attributed across multiple areas in an athlete's life. A swimmer might fail at meeting his goal times in two of his four events, but that doesn't mean he's a failure as a swimmer or as a person.

Changeable means that something can be done differently next time to produce a positive or different result. Focusing on failure as temporary, local, and changeable can help your athlete build resilience.

Psychologists Robert Sinclair and Janelle Cheung did an extensive review of the psychological literature and identified five overarching attributes that also influence resilience.[3] These attributes can be summarized by the acronym POWER.

P IS FOR PURPOSE: A sense of purpose provides internal motivation that an athlete needs to drive behaviors and make choices that lead to success. An athlete with a strong sense of purpose and clarity around why he plays his sport is more likely to bounce back from adversity. Purpose is not only about winning or excelling at a sport; it also can include the experiences of learning, mastering skills, contributing to a team, and developing leadership skills.

O IS FOR OPTIMISM: Dr. Seligman's decades of clinical research found that optimism is a skill that can be learned by managing negative self-talk and challenging assumptions about failure. According to Seligman, optimism is born from a belief that an individual can impact the outcome of a situation with effort. Optimism is not simply a belief that everything will be all right, nor is it about wearing rose-colored glasses. An optimist believes that he has the capacity to achieve a better result in the future with applied effort.

W IS FOR WILLPOWER: Willpower—a driving sense of commitment and determination—is often the secret ingredient for athletes. Yet, in times of doubt and distress, even the most accomplished athlete may struggle to find willpower. Walter Mischel, a Stanford University researcher, conducted a famous study in which preschoolers were given a choice between eating a marshmallow right away or waiting and holding out for a greater reward. Hundreds of hours of observation revealed that the strategies the children used to focus their attention determined whether they gave in to the temptation of the immediate reward or whether they were able to harness their willpower to wait for the greater reward.[4] Similarly, athletes who develop abilities to strategically focus their attention after setbacks are better able to access the willpower that drives resilience.

E IS FOR EMOTIONAL STABILITY: Emotional regulation promotes stability and resilience. When an athlete is triggered by adversity and gets emotionally hijacked, he cannot refocus and reset. The laser-focus demanded by elite performance can usually be attained only when mind and body are grounded and centered. Performing at highly competitive levels requires athletes to harness focus to perform consistently.

R IS FOR RESOURCEFULNESS: Resourceful thinking and the ability to identify a path forward allows athletes to navigate challenges more effectively. It has also been shown to reduce stress. Unfortunately, people in Gen Z (born after 1996) are more likely to struggle with resourcefulness.[5] They are growing up in an era when technology provides immediate answers to any question. It also connects them to parents who can provide immediate help. These factors may prevent

Gen Zers from having opportunities to solve practical problems that can build resilience.

As a parent, you can help your athlete cultivage the attributes in POWER by exploring these perspectives when he is struggling to bounce back from a failure. If he can develop the mindset and skills needed to emerge from setbacks, he will be resilient and positioned to grow as a high-performing athlete.

What gets in the way?

We want to gently remind you that parents with the best of intentions sometimes inadvertently derail their child's capacity for resilience. It is human nature for parents to feel protective when they witness their child experiencing a painful setback. It is common to want to jump in, pump up a child's confidence, and alleviate his pain and uncertainty.

You can reflect on whether you might occasionally fall into this pattern of protectiveness without even realizing you are doing so. Have you ever found yourself saying, "You'll beat them next time!" after your athlete suffers a particularly disappointing defeat? Or maybe you have told him, "You'll come back stronger," after a season-ending injury, or perhaps, "The coach just doesn't get you," when he failed to make the starting roster.

It is natural, normal, and common for a parent to make reassuring comments to help deflect a child's pain. Yet, it's critically important for you to recognize that such protective responses can work against both you and your athlete.

Protective responses can cost you priceless opportunities to help your athlete learn to tolerate and grow from setbacks and failures, which are at the heart of building resilience—and the foundation for success in most realms in life. Second, if your athlete sees you trying to immediately deflect or brush off his pain, he may think you are uncomfortable with his failure. He may become reluctant to be honest and less likely to share his disappointments. And over the years, he may begin to feel that he needs to be perfect—a mindset that definitely inhibits resilience and a growth orientation.

Third, protective and reassuring responses can create false assurances. To say "you deserved the starting spot" or "you're really the best at this position" might be an effort to pump up his confidence, but elite athletes are astute and can tell if there is a lack of congruence between what you say and the feedback he's getting from other sources.

A better approach is to sit quietly, listen intently to what your athlete tells you, remain neutral, and ask open-ended questions to help him process any disappointment he might be feeling.

Most parents act with the best of intentions to help prepare their children for reaching their potential and developing the fortitude to overcome difficulties. Early in your child's athletic career, you probably helped him set expectations about his performance and the work he would need to do to grow and improve.

Your role in your athlete's life will change as he rises to more elite levels of competition. At the highest levels, coaches and teammates typically fill the role of setting expectations about performance and effort. For many elite athletes, the real-world consequences of their performance become literal accountability measures. This shift can create intense pressure for developing athletes, and at these times they benefit from a parent's unconditional support and acceptance.

Athletes often talk about the challenges of the constant scrutiny they experience at elite levels. Knowing that he won't lose your love, pride in him, or support, whether he makes it or not at this level, is the lifeblood of healthy enduring relationships. This knowledge will help him weather the challenges of elite competition.

We know that the way parents talk to their athletes becomes a template for how athletes eventually talk to themselves. Compassionate self-talk increases resilience and performance outcomes in contrast to perfectionistic or self-destructive self-talk.[6] We aren't saying that you need to tip-toe around your athlete and gingerly approach every conversation. But being mindful of how you talk to him, and offering a compassionate approach by being loving, normalizing his feelings, and giving him perspective, will help him meet the high demands set by coaches and teammates.

The critical role you play in letting your athlete know that you are there for him first and foremost as a human being, rather than just as a high-performing athlete, cannot be overestimated.

Unconditional love is the one thing you alone can offer your child.

How can you help your athlete?

Listening and asking questions can be particularly useful when helping your athlete understand a failure. Instead of simply trying to reassure your child that he will get through a painful experience, you can help him think about it strategically so that he sees it as temporary, local, and changeable.

Imagine your son calls you after a long and grueling try-out process that ended poorly for him. You can start by acknowledging his sadness and disappointment. Help him calm down and regain his emotional balance. This may take days. When he is ready, you can then begin the process of deconstructing failure by first asking him what he did well. Typically, a failure does not mean that every action involved was wrong or bad. Failures often result from a few critical missteps. Helping him decipher what he did well and what he could have done better is the first step to seeing failure as "local."

Next, take the pulse of the conversation to see if your athlete is willing to discuss the situation further. If you sense he is open to going deeper, you can ask questions to help him see what contributed to the failure. Was it a lack of preparation? A problem of endurance? Underdeveloped skills? Nerves? Poor timing? Misread cues? A misunderstanding of expectations? Through this process, your athlete can reflect on what contributed to the failure, so he can identify what he has control over and where he can apply effort moving forward.

At this point, it is valuable to have him check-in with his intuition. You might ask when he had a hunch that things were not going well. For example, he might have noticed that something shifted, and he lost the coach's attention a couple of hours into the tryouts. This insight might help him realize that his defensive skills were not as strong as they could have been. Or, perhaps he sees that he never felt good, and the problem was in his preparation two days before tryouts. The goal here is to help your athlete review the process and learn to spot red flags so that he can read situations better and prepare differently next time. These steps help him to see failure as temporary and as a situation that he can overcome if he approaches things differently in the future.

Finally, helping your child think strategically about failure cultivates optimism. Again, remember that optimism is the belief that with concerted effort, he can do things differently to positively impact future outcomes. Where and how your athlete directs his concerted effort makes all the difference.

It can be a natural default to blame the coach, make excuses for a poor performance, or justify a difficult outcome. Yet these behaviors remove any personal responsibility for change and inhibit a growth mindset. If you find your child easily defaults to blame or excuses, consider what he might feel the need to protect. Does he feel vulnerable when he makes a mistake? Does he feel pressure to be the best? Does he have to live up to an image people have of him? Understanding what might motivate him to blame others or make excuses can help you work with him to better tolerate these uncomfortable experiences. You will read more about these very natural but limiting behaviors in the next chapter.

Strategies in Action

Imagine your son is recovering from a shoulder injury and is not able to start the tennis season. The journey back from surgery has been difficult, and he is frustrated with his progress. He calls you wondering if he should quit and be done with tennis. It is his senior year. He is worried that if his shoulder is not better soon, he will miss his final season. At the same time, he is questioning whether playing again is worth the time and pain of physical therapy. He says to you, "It's my last year of college, and I've given all my time and energy to tennis." He has dreamed of an NCAA championship for years and was so close to accomplishing the goal before the injury. You are worried he will quit, and the thought devastates you.

PARENT: Do you regret giving so much time and energy to tennis?

SON: No, not really. I'm just frustrated. This isn't how it was supposed to be.

PARENT: It's certainly not what you planned for. I can only imagine how disappointing this continues to be.

SON: I just don't know if I have it in me to push through this and get back on the court.

PARENT: It's hard to stay energized when you're not getting the rewards of competing and excelling.

SON: What do you think I should do?

PARENT: This is a hard decision, and one that only you can make. Maybe it will help to think of this. Imagine looking back at yourself three years from now. What decision would you like to be able to say you made?

SON: I'd like to be able to say I stuck it out, came back, and won the championship. But it's not that easy. I could stick it out and this injury could still be a problem.

PARENT: True. Three years from now, what might you regret?

SON: Hmmm—I think I'd regret not trying to come back. I have been reaching for this my whole life. I just wish I felt more energized and inspired right now.

PARENT: So, it sounds like you would regret not persevering, and that if things could work out perfectly, you'd come back and have a shot at winning. But the issue is finding the energy and will to work through this rehab.

SON: That is exactly it.

PARENT: When do you feel the most down and frustrated?

SON: After I work out and my shoulder is throbbing. I don't mind going to work out. I think it's when it hurts afterward. I freak out and wonder if it is ever going to get better.

PARENT: So, working through the anxiety and pain is the hard part, not finding the will to push yourself.

SON: Yeah, I hadn't really thought about it this way.

PARENT: What might you do to get support for this part of the recovery?

SON: I guess I could talk to our trainer about it. He mentioned that I might connect with the university's sports psychologist, but I never did that.

PARENT: If you could meet with the sports psychologist, what would you like to ask her?

SON: I'd like to know if this is normal stress I feel about my shoulder. It's like I don't know how to trust my body now. I always would push through pain, and it was okay. Now, I worry that if I push through this, I'm damaging it more.

PARENT: I bet she'd be able to provide some valuable insights. She might also be able to share other tips for bouncing back from this surgery. When can you make an appointment?

SON: I'll call the trainer tomorrow to see how I get in to see her.

In this conversation, the parent stayed calm and did not introduce his own anxiety about his son quitting. He resisted giving advice and allowed his son to explore his own deeper feelings about the situation. To help with this, the parent asked questions for his son to reflect on the consequences and potential regrets of the decisions he was contemplating. He also helped his son unpack the challenges and reexamine priorities. Because the parent stayed on the sidelines and let his son do the talking, feeling, and thinking, his son was able to identify contributing factors to the problem and create a plan of action.

We close this chapter with a story about Sian Leah Beilock, a former competitive soccer player who currently serves as the president of Barnard College. Beilock was the goalie for the Olympic Development Program's California State team. In her TED Talk, she shares a story about a particular game when she was playing very well until she realized the national coach was standing behind her evaluating her performance. At this moment, she fell apart. She suddenly found herself bobbling the ball and feeling as if things were moving in slow motion. Her performance started to unravel. And then she choked. Instead of knocking a shot away, she tipped it right into her own goal.

As frustrating as this moment was, the experience ignited a lifelong passion to understand why humans choke under pressure. She went on to get doctorate degrees in psychology and kinesiology. In her book, *Choke: What the Secrets of the Brain Reveal about Getting It Right When You Have To,* Dr. Beilock writes about how brain and body functions can cause us to choke under pressure, whether in sports, job interviews, test-taking, or public speaking. She also discusses strategies to overcome tendencies to fall apart in stressful situations, including practicing regularly under stressful conditions, watching for behavior contagion in groups that exacerbates stress, and journaling to download worrisome thoughts. If your athlete tends to choke under pressure and would like to improve his resilience, he might benefit from reading Dr. Beilock's work or listening to her TED Talk.

Conversation Questions

To wrap up, we offer these questions for you to ask your athlete when the types of situations described in this Pillar arise.

- *What went well in this situation?*

- *What contributed to this failure or setback?*

- *When did you first suspect things weren't going well?*

- *If you could go back to that moment, what corrective action could you have taken?*

- *Where can you focus as you move forward to achieve a different outcome?*

- *What do you want to be able to say about this experience three years from now?*

Questions for Your Reflection

What might your child need to hear from you when he fails or faces setbacks?

_____

_____

How do you handle your own sense of disappointment when you witness your child's setbacks and struggles?

_____

_____

What does unconditional support for your child look like to you?

_____

_____

When have you witnessed a parent handle a child's setbacks well, and what would you like to emulate?

_____

_____

Show Up Ready to Receive and Process Feedback

Many of you have heard the claim that mastering a skill requires 10,000 hours of practice. However, not all practice is equal. Practice infused with mistakes, and without intentional learning, will not lead to mastery.

Psychologist K. Anders Ericsson uses the term smart practice to describe the process that leads to mastery.[1] Smart practice is not simply about repetition, but about repeatedly adjusting execution. For example, smart practice of a tennis serve might include honing in on trouble spots, such as the ball toss, and working on this specific element, rather than repeating the same serve over and over. Or, an elite figure skater might isolate and focus on the most challenging 20 seconds of her program rather than skating her entire routine again and again.

One of the most critical components of developing smart practice habits is the ability to use feedback effectively. Feedback loops, whether generated by coaches, teammates, or self-reflection, give an athlete information that can be used to improve. At its essence, feedback is information. Yet, how it is delivered can make all the difference in how an athlete responds.

Unfortunately, the way feedback is delivered often lands outside of an athlete's control. Some coaches are skilled at giving feedback, but some are not. Some coaches scream from the sidelines and others give it in one-on-one meetings or group huddles. And in the heat of competition, feedback can be brutally direct and harsh. While receiving feedback can be difficult for even the most seasoned professional, athletes benefit by being able to process different styles of feedback from different sources.

It's important for an athlete to learn to hear feedback with a growth mindset. If your athlete can respond with a "Thank you–tell me more attitude" and perceive the feedback not as a personal attack but as a critical component in her progress towards mastery, she is more likely to be able to grow in her performance skills.

One way to help your athlete learn to receive feedback with a growth mindset is to talk with her about self-compassion and the role it can play in processing difficult feedback. Most people are their own harshest critics, and difficult feedback can easily dissolve into destructive, negative self-talk. You can help your athlete to be mindful of her internal voice and guide her in learning to talk to herself in a compassionate, growth-oriented tone that provides wisdom and perspective.

What does your child usually say to herself in the face of hard-to-hear feedback? If she thinks along the lines of "I screwed up and lost the game," or "I'm terrible at fast breaks," she is engaging in negative self-talk. If, instead, she can learn to tell herself, "I'm learning and growing," "Mistakes are part of the process," or "I'm developing my skills," then she will have the language to combat negative self-talk. Self-compassion isn't about coddling or deflecting painful information; it's about strengthening the resiliency an athlete needs to effectively utilize critical information and develop in the right ways.

What gets in the way?

Feedback can feel threatening to an athlete if it comes across as a personal attack, judgment of her abilities, or a comment on her work. Feedback can also feel punitive. For some elite athletes, feedback that feels threatening or judgmental triggers the emotional alarm system, and makes it hard to listen and learn. In these situations, your athlete is likely to feel bad about herself or angry at the messenger, instead of being open to seeing the information as a tool for improving. Even the most growth-minded people can fall into a defensive or defeated state in the face of criticism.

Some athletes have more practice dealing with feedback than others. An athlete who has been blessed with natural talent may have advanced athletically for years receiving little criticism. However, there comes a time for most athletes at elite levels of competition when they find themselves in situations where they are suddenly pushed by critical feedback. Additionally, these athletes may have enjoyed practice in the past, but at the elite levels find themselves discouraged by the expected level of performance. This can challenge their confidence, and they might shut down or simply ignore what they hear, creating problems on multiple levels. These situations offer the opportunity to embrace the discomfort that accompanies growth.

Openly receiving feedback is the first step to leveraging it as an opportunity to raise awareness and identify actions for improvement. It is about learning to hear the content of the message, rather than reacting to how it is delivered. You can remind your athlete that feedback from coaches typically signals confidence in her ability to improve. In fact, feedback is often an endorsement of potential.

Receiving feedback gracefully is a skill that takes time and practice. An athlete also needs maturity and personal accountability to be able to process and act upon feedback effectively. We like to talk about accountability in terms of behavior that is above the line or below the line.

Above-the-line behaviors include listening and processing information from coaches and teammates, asking questions for clarification, adjusting one's approach based on feedback, and taking ownership of one's choices and mistakes. Above-the-line behaviors also include nonverbal or verbal acknowledgment during practice or games, signaling that the feedback was received. Staying above the line with such behaviors keeps athletes in a growth mindset and a process-oriented approach.

Below-the-line behaviors include blaming, justifying, excusing, or denying. These reactions are common ways that people protect their ego and self-esteem and can be instinctive reactions in an athlete who feels attacked or misunderstood. The problem, however, is that below-the-line behaviors render an athlete powerless and feeling like a victim of circumstance. By deflecting responsibility, below-the-line behaviors rob her of the opportunity to focus on what is within her control for growth and improvement.

Here are examples of below-the-line behaviors that often show up when an athlete is given difficult feedback.

BLAME: Blame happens when an athlete deflects responsibility for something that happened by assigning it to someone else. This might sound like an athlete saying, "if the back line held their positions, this would have never happened." Blame shifts responsibility to another source completely outside of the athlete's control.

JUSTIFICATION: Justifying happens when an athlete looks for ways to explain why she made a certain choice. Again, it can be a way of deflecting the pain of receiving criticism. For example, a softball centerfielder, who was out of position on an easy fly ball and missed the catch, might say to the coach, "I moved toward second base because I thought I could catch the ball and make a double play." Athletes may justify their choices to show they had good intentions. They likely want a coach or teammate to know they meant well and were doing what they thought was right. However, coaches do not want to hear explanations every time they correct a player. In the moment, they may not care why an athlete did what she did or about the intentions behind it. They simply want her to make the adjustment or correction. Mature athletes know that it is their job to accept the feedback, and that repeatedly justifying actions comes across as defensive. If an athlete is confused about corrective feedback, it is a great opportunity for her to practice managing up to get greater clarification.

EXCUSES: Athletes can fall into the trap of making excuses when things go poorly. Excuses involve placing the responsibility of an outcome on some extenuating circumstances like an injury, bad weather, or not feeling well. Of course, all these things can impact an athlete's performance. But excuses too often become a crutch to regularly explain what happens when things do not go well. In these cases, excuses get in the way of an athlete taking ownership and identifying what she can do differently to improve.

DENIAL: Denial happens when an athlete fails to accept the reality of feedback. She might say, "I wasn't out of position," or "I did what you said," or "I didn't slow up before the finish line." A denial response can happen when an athlete truly sees things differently than the person giving feedback, or when she finds the feedback too painful or shameful to accept in the moment.

For each of these feedback deflections, you can help your child by gently guiding her to a broader perspective to see where in the situation she can assume some control. A simple question such as "What small changes could you make next time to lead to a different outcome?" can put her in a place of ownership. Again, it's not about accepting every piece of feedback wholesale, but rather helping her decipher the information so she can use it to make conscious choices that will help her grow as an elite athlete.

Learning how to distinguish between useful and not so useful feedback will help your athlete to process and maximize its impact. A good strategy is to invite your athlete to consider who is offering the message. Is it coming from a coach, trainer, teammate, fans, the media, or a family member? What level of expertise does the person giving feedback have? Does the individual have direct knowledge of all the relevant circumstances? One of the most important questions she can ask herself is, "Does this individual have my best interests at heart?"

If an athlete receives feedback that raises a red flag or does not feel right, she might want to pause, step away from the individual giving the feedback, and take time to process it. Creating temporary distance can be particularly helpful if she receives a challenging message from a teammate. Stepping away can lower the 'emotional volume' and help her to see a situation from a broader perspective. She may then need to initiate a conversation with the person supplying the feedback to gain further clarification or launch a deeper discussion.

One final topic to mention in this section is the long tradition of coaches using shame, contempt, harsh criticism, and fear to motivate athletes. These tactics can successfully change short-term behaviors but often fail to motivate athletes in the long run. And they often lead to a loss of trust and respect for the individual displaying this kind of behavior.

Negative motivational strategies are often unconsciously used to deflect the deliverer's own personal frustration, anger, and insecurities. They can negatively impact performance by shutting down communication lines and making it difficult for the athlete to listen and respond positively to any message being delivered. If you see your child in a situation such as this, use the strategies outlined below to help her distance herself emotionally and manage the feedback in a way that will support her growth and development.

How can you help your athlete?

The process of helping your athlete work with feedback involves three parts: awareness, action, and accountability. Remember that your role is to facilitate her reflection process and NOT to offer up your own opinion of the feedback. It's important that you remain neutral; if you join up with your athlete emotionally, it can easily shift the conversation to being about you. Instead, start with an acknowledging statement that shows you understand and empathize with her feelings or experience, something along the lines of, "I can see it's upsetting to hear this feedback," or "I can see the coach's criticism is discouraging for you." These statements help you diffuse the intensity of the emotions she may be feeling, and this in turn will help her open up and increase her awareness. As we mentioned earlier, it is nearly impossible to learn and process information when overcome by anger and other intense emotions.

Awareness

Begin by asking, "What is the essence of the feedback?" This question creates an opportunity for her to distill and summarize what she has heard. It also helps create distance from the message, the context in which it was delivered, and the messenger.

You can also remind your athlete to "listen to learn" and stay curious. While this can be challenging when a coach is yelling at her, she can emotionally distance herself with the question, "What can I learn from this?" This question can shift her perspective and keep her from getting defensive and feeling defeated. It also puts the power in her hands by focusing on what she can learn.

One final step for creating awareness around feedback is asking your child, "What rings true about this information?" Invite her to sit with the message and try it on to see if it fits.

Action

If the feedback makes sense to your child, you can encourage action by asking, "How might things be different if you apply what you are hearing?" or "How will acting on this information make you a better player, teammate, or person?" or "What support do you need to make this change?" These questions put her in the driver's seat; it will be up to her to take action and move forward.

Of course, understanding whether feedback rings true is not always straightforward. For example, feedback about being in the wrong position during a breakaway play does not require much processing time to determine if it lands well or not. It is fairly objective. It can be a different story when larger issues arise, such as feedback that your athlete will never play at the Division I collegiate level. When the situation is big, you can encourage your athlete to take the time to sit with the message and figure out her best response and course of action.

There may be times when your athlete completely disagrees with the feedback she receives. Helping her clarify why she disagrees will assist her in working through the experience. Often, feedback can ring untrue when it conflicts with other messages she may have received. Conflicting messages can leave an athlete frustrated and uncertain. When this happens, help your athlete identify where the different messages fail to align, and then encourage her to take action by initiating conversations to clarify the intent of the feedback.

Many coaches deliver instantaneous feedback, and a player must respond in mid-stride. When this happens and the feedback is confusing, it provides an excellent opportunity for her to be proactive after the practice or game by asking for a meeting to discuss it in greater detail. Doing this can help her not only understand what she needs to do differently, but also how she can implement this knowledge moving forward.

Accountability

After creating awareness and a plan of action, you can discuss personal accountability. When an athlete holds herself accountable for implementing appropriate feedback, she builds credibility with both coaches and teammates. This is a key component of being coachable. When she resists holding herself accountable and moves to a place of blame, excuses, and justifications, she deflects personal responsibility and surrenders her power to strategically improve. The important point is not to create shame when excuses or blame get in the way of her ownership. Instead, gently nudge her to see what might be possible if she takes action.

Again, if your athlete tends to resist feedback, remind her that it is a sign that coaches are watching and investing in her development. Receiving feedback often means that she is on the coaches' radar, which is usually a positive thing.

Finally, encourage your athlete to practice asking for and receiving feedback when appropriate. Kim Scott, author of *Radical Candor,* shared that former Google executive Fred Kofman solicits feedback regularly by asking: "What can I start or stop doing to make it easier to work (play, live, coach) with me?"[2] Athletes can learn a lot by asking their coaches and teammates this question.

To close, we offer a few thoughts on athletes receiving feedback from parents. As we mentioned earlier, it can be challenging to give feedback as a parent because you may not have full knowledge of the coach-player relationship or the team dynamic. This lack of knowledge can lead to irrelevant or faulty perspectives. You might ask yourself if you have enough information about a situation to give accurate, effective feedback. You might also consider that when athletes get conflicting feedback from coaches and parents it can lead to divided loyalties and create anxiety. If you do decide to share your perspective, it can be helpful to acknowledge that you may be missing important information that could impact the message you are offering.

There are certainly times a parent's perspective can be hugely beneficial, especially when the timing and content of the message are on target. By offering compassion, perspective, and understanding while delivering feedback, your athlete will be more receptive to your message.

Here are a few questions you might consider about yourself before you offer your perspective to your child.

- When is it hard for you to receive feedback from others?

- When is it easy to receive feedback from others?

- What helps you to stay open to hearing difficult feedback?

After reflecting on the above questions, take a moment to consider the following:

- How does your child typically receive feedback from you?

- What might help her be open to your message? (For example, would she be more open if she hears it alone without an audience, in a neutral and nonemotional tone of voice, or with a greater context of your perspective.)

- What might she need to hear from you, in addition to your feedback, to help her process your message? (For example, an acknowledgement of her effort or an empathetic statement for how she might be feeling.)

- What do you want her to know about your intentions?

One final thought: any opportunity you have to demonstrate receiving feedback gracefully yourself in front of your child gives her an experience to see the process in action. It doesn't matter if the feedback comes from a professional colleague, a boss, or a friend. And if your child can't witness the exchange in real time, you can certainly share your experience with her in a conversation. Nothing can be more helpful than the role modeling you provide.

In the next chapter, you will read about a tactical process for giving feedback that both you and your athlete can practice.

Strategies in Action

We will return to the example above of an athlete receiving feedback that she will never succeed at the Division I collegiate level. There is perhaps no harder message to hear for an athlete than not having what it takes to remain competitive at the next level. Having a supportive parent to help process this feedback can make all the difference in an athlete's experience.

DAUGHTER: Coach said my chances of getting recruited by a DI school are slim to nothing.

PARENT: Wow, I'm guessing that isn't the feedback you wanted to hear. How do you feel about that?

DAUGHTER: Mad, like she doesn't know what she's talking about.

PARENT: I bet.

DAUGHTER: She's never believed in me.

PARENT: What do you want to do about it?

DAUGHTER: What can I do?

PARENT: Do you believe her?

DAUGHTER: She doesn't get me. She doesn't know what I can do. That's been half my struggle with this team. I haven't had the playing time to prove myself.

PARENT: I understand how frustrated you were last season. What do you think Coach is missing about you?

DAUGHTER: She doesn't know how hard I work. How hard I train on my own. How willing I am to do what it takes.

PARENT: How did you respond when the coach told you she doesn't think you had what it takes to play Division I?

DAUGHTER: I didn't say anything. I stayed quiet.

PARENT: If you could have a very honest conversation with Coach about this, what would you want her to know?

DAUGHTER: How important this is to me and how hard I'm willing to work at it.

PARENT: What would you want to know from her?

DAUGHTER: I'd want to know why she thinks I can't make it. I know I'm small but I'm not the smallest player she's ever had that went DI. I guess I'd want to know what she'd do if she were me and wanted this more than anything.

PARENT: It sounds like you'd like some specifics—some concrete things you could do to be seen differently by her and DI recruiters.

DAUGHTER: That'd be helpful. I know she has a lot of experience. But she could be wrong about me. I want to prove her wrong.

PARENT: So, what would it look like if you asked Coach for a meeting and told her you'd like her help in proving her wrong. That you'd like a few things you could do on the field, in practice, and with your mental game that could make a difference this season. How do you think she'd respond?

DAUGHTER: Deep down, I think she'd respect me. I even wonder if she is looking for me to push back on this. To see how committed I am.

PARENT: What will happen if you ask for the meeting, do all the work, and you still don't get recruited?

DAUGHTER: It's better than not fighting at all.

PARENT: Then go for it.

There is no doubt that receiving negative feedback can be hard and painful. Yet, many successful athletes say their successes have been fueled by difficult feedback. You can help your athlete process what she can learn from these experiences so that she can stay above the line and advance her growth as an athlete and person.

We close this chapter with insights Serena Williams shared in 2019 during a keynote speech for the technology company, Slack. She noted that while tennis used to be considered an individual sport, success in this arena requires serious team collaboration. Nutritionists, trainers, and other highly specialized individuals must work together in support of a unified mission. When collaborating with her team, she said that of all the tools in her toolkit, soliciting feedback is perhaps the most powerful. Pursuing feedback propelled her to greatness in tennis and continues to serve her as the founder of Serena Ventures, a firm committed to investing in founders and products positioned to change the world. "I tell my coach and my fashion team, don't tell me what I'm doing right," Williams says, "I want to hear what I'm doing wrong so I can improve and become better."[3] In her current role helping companies succeed, she commits to giving feedback to ensure they operate in alignment with their mission.

When asked why feedback is so important to her, Serena responds, "There's someone working just as hard as me, if not harder. They're trying to beat me, and I need to always stay a step above." Feedback, it appears, continues to be a critical tool for maintaining her competitive edge.

Conversation Questions

To wrap up, we offer these questions for you to ask your athlete when the types of situations described in this Pillar arise.

- *What's the essence of this information?*

- *What resonates with you? What doesn't?*

- *What might you learn from this information?*

- *What confuses you about this feedback?*

- *What would help you process and grow from this information?*

- *What are you willing to do with this feedback?*

Questions for Your Reflection

How does your child experience and manage negative self-talk?

_____

_____

When might your child fall into "below-the-line" behaviors?

_____

_____

How do you decide when it is useful to give your child feedback?
What contributes to successful or problematic interactions?

_____

_____

What helps you to process difficult feedback?

_____

_____

PILLAR 9

Show Up for Your Team

In the previous chapter, we discussed personal accountability and how it relates to an athlete's ability to receive and process feedback. Without personal accountability, it is impossible to assume the ownership required for serious growth and development. At the same time, athletic teams can only evolve and grow when players extend personal accountability to team accountability.

The choices athletes make on and off the field to show up prepared to do their best for the team are at the heart of team accountability. How they support one another directly during practice and competition influences the team dynamic. The choices they make about sleeping, eating, and managing their emotions impact team performance.

Because of the stress and demands placed on elite athletes, emotions can run high and easily be transferred to others on a team. Emotions are contagious and can impact even the highest-performing teams.[1] Negative attitudes about a coach can be infectious, and one player's disbelief in a team's ability to overcome a series of losses can sweep through the group. Such contagion can be hard to manage and has profound consequences. A big part of athletes showing up for their teams goes back to the discussion about managing emotions in a positive, healthy manner.

Leadership expert Jon Gordon and motivational speaker Damon West use the metaphor of a coffee bean to help athletes understand the transformative power of their emotions.[2] They talk about experiences that can feel like a pot of boiling water and how these experiences can weaken, harden, or transform people. Gordon and West ask athletes to consider carrots which become soft in boiling water, eggs which harden in boiling water, and coffee beans which transform boiling water. Understanding that attitudes and emotions have the power to transform a group, much like coffee beans transform boiling water, is at the heart of this Pillar.

It's not just emotions and attitudes that are contagious, but behaviors as well. Behavioral contagion both positively and negatively impacts team culture. Earlier, we referenced the story of Michael Jordan using his emotions of frustration and disappointment to fuel his commitment to grow and develop on the court. In fact, his college coaches credited the contagion of his work ethic as a major factor in the team's success. Jordan's relentless drive to improve became infectious and created a culture of hard work and perseverance that positively impacted the team's performance.

The opposite can just as easily happen, especially when collegiate athletes may be living on their own for the first time, and their choices outside of athletics can negatively impact team culture and performance. Athletes need to be mindful of their own potentially contagious behaviors, and they may need to address teammates' behaviors that are negatively impacting the overall culture. If your athlete finds themself on a team where behaviors such as late-night gaming and partying are becoming contagious and hurting performance, they may not be able to immediately influence everyone's actions. However, you can remind them that they can impact the culture over time by making healthy choices for themself whenever possible.

One challenge with developing team accountability stems from the extreme emphasis placed on an individual's growth in their early athletic career. Collegiate athletes who grew up playing for competitive club programs, where there is an organizational mission to groom individual talent, often talk about the transition from a group of high-performing individual athletes to an environment with a greater team orientation. Yet, even teams with a strong collective orientation experience some inherent competition within the ranks. Players compete for starting positions, opportunities to score, and All-Star invitations. However, when teams coalesce and experience cohesion around the tasks required for high performance, they have a greater chance of outperforming teams with members who don't work well together.[3] In addition, when athletes perceive that they are part of a team that works well together, they report higher levels of satisfaction and enjoyment.[4]

Creating high levels of team cohesion requires a shift of focus from "I" to "we." It calls for athletes to consider the greater good of the team and to adopt a service orientation by asking themselves, "What can I do to help the team perform at its best?"

A study of nearly 200 high school basketball athletes in the Pacific Northwest found that when coaches showed up as servant leaders, with actions grounded in trust, humility, service, and inclusion, athletes displayed higher intrinsic motivation, greater mental agility, a healthier psychological profile, and better overall performance.[5] One can only imagine the impact when players show up as servant leaders for their fellow teammates.

The corporate world also recognizes servant leadership as a key performance enhancer. According to a recent McKinsey quarterly report, a servant leader disposition bolsters team performance by increasing innovation and joint problem-solving, reducing absenteeism, and enhancing productivity.[6] The report suggested that business managers ask themselves, "How do I make my team members' lives easier—physically, cognitively, and emotionally?" Athletes who consider this same question are more likely to show up fully for their teams and to reap equally positive results.

For athletes, servant leadership can look like actions as simple as picking up discarded trash after a team meal, carrying extra equipment when the team travels, or helping a team manager refill water bottles. Or, it can look like reaching out to a new teammate who seems lonely or initiating a group discussion to manage team conflict. Players might also consciously choose to impact team culture by challenging negative team talk.

Service to others requires a sense of humility. Concern for the team takes precedence over an individual's needs or ego, and this leadership shift can be challenging. Yet, when athletes learn to do this, it can expand their influence and lead to great results in and out of sports.

What gets in the way?

In our work with athletes and coaches, we have identified three major factors that prevent athletes from showing up for their team. One problem arises when athletes see themselves as separate from the team; they may perceive themselves as being either more or less skilled than the other players, and therefore either more or less worthy of being on the team.

An athlete who is a star player can have a profound impact on a team. If a star player is a role model with a stellar work ethic who mentors rising players on the team, their leadership can dramatically elevate the entire team's performance. On the other hand, if a star player slacks off or expects special privileges, they lose the opportunity to help the team develop—and may even create animosity. Helping your athlete see the leadership opportunity inherent in being a star performer and truly showing up for the team with a sense of servitude provides invaluable life lessons. At the same time, it may be helpful for your child to remember that athletes develop at different rates. A struggling performer one year can be the star the next year.

What if your athlete does not possess the same skills as their teammates and feels unworthy of being on the team? In this case, it can be helpful for them to reflect on the big picture and remember that because athletes develop at different rates, much like they physically grow at different rates, their rank on a team is not necessarily fixed forever. An athlete in this situation can focus on what they can control to improve their abilities and benefit from assessing other ways they bring value to the team. Do they have a positive, contagious spirit that boosts team morale? Do they have a work ethic that sets a standard for the team? Or perhaps, they have the social savvy that keeps the team dynamics positive and fluid. Coaches often look to players who possess interpersonal strengths to provide team leadership and create a positive culture in the locker room.

Another factor that interferes with a player's ability to show up fully for their team is a sense of entitlement. Entitlement can result when an athlete's expectations are not met, and they do not have the support or ability to work through disappointment. For example, consider a player's sense of disappointment after losing an expected starting role on the team. Without taking the steps to work through the disappointment, the athlete might fall into negative behavior that undermines the coach and fellow players. Such behaviors in turn negatively impact team cohesion.

Disappointment in sports is real and to be expected. It is an integral part of high-stakes competition. However, the way a player manages disappointment makes all the difference. The athlete who processes their feelings with the right people at the right time, resists speaking negatively to teammates about the situation, works with the coach to discover areas for improvement, and continues to be of service to the team, will be better positioned to avoid the entitlement trap and positively evolve from disappointment.

As a parent, you might be the person your child turns to for processing disappointment. Again, your ability to remain neutral in such situations will be critical so that they can acknowledge the pain and work through their feelings. Ultimately this will help them choose behaviors that will serve them well in the long run.

A third factor that negatively impacts team accountability is poorly managed conflict. While research shows that conflict is a natural part of team dynamics, it can destroy teams if not managed well. Once a team is divided, internal fighting wastes precious focus and energy that could otherwise be channeled toward the opponent. Overcoming conflict to show up fully for the team is a big task and can be particularly challenging for an athlete fighting a negative team dynamic.

Teams move through cycles, some of which are more susceptible to conflict than others. According to psychologist Bruce Tuckman, teams typically experience five stages of development.[7] The first stage is forming when teams come together. In this stage, relationships are being built and the team culture is being established. Excitement is generally high, and anticipation is great. Teams then evolve to the second stage, storming, when they are tested and may face disappointments. Personality clashes often occur as people become more comfortable with the group and conflicts arise. The third stage, norming, is when team members coalesce and begin to identify systems for working together.

The fourth stage, performing, happens when teams work together productively and the members push one another to grow. In this stage, feedback flows freely and effectively. Players have adjusted to their positions, leaders have stepped into their roles, and the group norms have been accepted. And while conflict may arise on performing teams, team members know how to move through it without detrimental impact. In this stage, teams are better able to manage setbacks and unexpected challenges. They are agile and able to make adjustments to continue performing at high levels.

The fifth and final stage, adjourning, happens when it is time for a team to disband. Athletes may experience grief or mourning when a team's time comes to an end. In this stage, it can be helpful to focus on the team's accomplishments and celebrate the overall growth.

Moving through these stages from forming to adjourning can be challenging. As a parent, you can play a constructive role by helping your athlete understand that these are predictable phases. As team members assume new roles and adjust to new norms, frustration can result. Players who were once underclassmen may now grapple with new leadership responsibilities, and other players may not be as readily open to such changes. New team norms may require an uncomfortable change in behavior. These adjustments take time and may create conflict, confusion, and resistance. And while this notion of team development may seem more relevant for team athletes than for individual athletes, there are often hierarchies and social dynamics in individual competition that need to be navigated.

How can you help your athlete?

If your athlete is on a team experiencing conflict, you can utilize the conversation strategies you have been reading about to help them manage the situation. For example, imagine your child is the captain of a team that is struggling at the start of the season. The head coach has been put on leave for disciplinary reasons. The interim coach has failed to earn the trust and respect of the players. The seniors, who had high expectations for the season, are feeling angry and cheated. The players have started to turn on one another and this has negatively impacted performance. Your athlete complains to you about the players and coaches and feels trapped by the spiraling situation. Incidentally, this often happens during an unexpected losing season as well. Both coaches and athletes can turn on each other to place blame.

A first step is to help them see what, if anything, they might have done or might be doing to contribute to the conflict. Second, you can help them imagine a greater vision of what might be possible for the team. To do this, revisit the questions offered by Aldo Civico, the former director of Columbia University's Center for International Conflict Resolution.[8] These questions, adapted and listed below, highlight what an athlete can control in the midst of strife. In a nutshell, Civico's questions can help your athlete redirect the conflict from a problem-based orientation to a solution-based one.

Instead of focusing solely on the problem, what is contributing to it, the limitations your child faces, and the parties at fault, offer up the following questions for consideration:

- How might you want to be different in this situation?
- What inner resources will support you in accomplishing this?
- How would a shift in your perspective impact you as a team leader and player?
- How might your being different impact the team overall?
- How might you look and sound when operating from this different place?
- How might you feel differently?

If your athlete is unsure of their role in resolving the conflict, you could ask:

- What do you see your role to be in this situation?
- What do you feel your responsibility is here?
- What part do you want to play in this situation?

These questions can elevate your athlete from feeling victimized by circumstances to experiencing choice, ownership, and possibility.

In addition to helping your athlete navigate team conflict, you can help them learn how to give effective feedback to teammates. This is a critical component of showing up fully for a team. In the previous chapter, we discussed receiving and processing feedback. We can look through the lens of showing up for your team to discuss how athletes can give feedback to one another effectively.

It is typical for athletes to yell at each other in the heat of the moment when emotions are running high. When the team culture is strong, individuals can absorb this natural tendency as being a part of the game. However, when the relationships are weak and trust is tenuous, knowing how to deliver more thoughtful feedback can be a critical asset for athletes, especially for team leaders.

To help your athlete develop this skill, share this three-step model introduced by the Center For Creative Leadership—**Situation, Behavior, Impact**.[9]

Identify the **situation** so the context is clear and specific. What did they observe happening? For this step, focus on a specific event that stands as a clear example. For example, a player on the team stayed out late the previous evening partying with a group of friends and broke curfew. As a result, this player was sluggish and not on their game.

Identify the specific **behavior** that you want to address. What specifically contributed to the problem? Look for actionable behaviors that can be changed. In this example, the player failed to hustle downfield during three breakaways, which kept them from being positioned to receive the ball in front of the undefended goal.

Identify the specific **impact** of the behavior. What happened as a result? This player was often out of position and cost the team multiple scoring opportunities which in turn contributed to losing the game.

Once these steps are outlined, your athlete can offer solutions for change if appropriate in the situation. When suggesting new actions, it is helpful to emphasize the new behavior that will lead to positive results, instead of focusing on removing the old behavior that led to poor outcomes. To continue with the above example, your athlete could say, "Taking care of yourself the night before games not only makes you a better player, it impacts all of us. When you show up ready to play, the team notices. You are quicker to the ball and the whole back line plays differently. It is going to take you committing to being at 100 percent for our team to reach our playoff dream."

In summary, when giving feedback it is best to:

- Keep the feedback focused on concrete behaviors. Don't attack the person's character!

- Emphasize what someone can do instead of what they shouldn't do or need to stop doing.

- Deliver the feedback in person and in a timely manner.

While it may be tempting for an athlete to send a text or throw out an off-hand comment a week after the event, the feedback will have far greater impact if they pull the player aside right after the game, look them in the eyes, and have an honest conversation. Conveying feedback with genuine intent to help someone improve or grow, as opposed to offering feedback from a place of judgment or anger, helps the message land better. So you might suggest your athlete take a moment to align their intentions before offering feedback by asking themself:

- What do I want to accomplish by delivering this message?

- How can I deliver the feedback in a way that preserves my teammate's dignity while challenging them to perform at a higher level?

- Am I calm enough right now to deliver this feedback effectively and thoughtfully?

Athletes can employ this strategy when giving individual or collective feedback to the team at large. To build this critical leadership skill, encourage your child to practice giving positive feedback. Learning to be specific with **situations, behaviors,** and **impacts** is a strategy that can be practiced just as easily when things go well, allowing them to hone the skill for great advantage.

A final way to promote this Pillar is to help your athlete see the value of fully committing to the team every day. This commitment requires embracing both the rights and the responsibilities of being on a team. The rights of being respected, having a voice, and having a safe space to practice and compete must be balanced with the responsibilities of having their teammates' backs and consistently putting the team first.

Athletes face tough choices every day. Sacrifice is part of every athlete's journey. Decisions as to whether they sleep in, stay out late with friends the night before a game, or to take a personal trip and miss a preseason practice can feel incidental to a less seasoned athlete, especially if they aren't the team's star. However, these decisions establish patterns and expectations for behaviors. And as we've mentioned, such behaviors can be contagious, impacting the team at large. Every choice each athlete makes regarding how they show up for one another impacts the team's fabric. Helping your athlete recognize their responsibility for the team's greater good will benefit them in the long run.

Strategies in Action

Imagine your athlete plays collegiate soccer. It is their junior year, and they have been a star performer. A recent knee injury has sidelined them for the remainder of the season. Your child calls home and mentions that going to practice and sitting on the sidelines is a waste of time. From what you hear, it sounds as if they are pulling away from the team. When you ask about goals for next year, they express wanting to be back in full force, and say they can't wait to return to competition.

> PARENT: What can you be doing now to help prepare you for next season?
>
> ATHLETE: Nothing. Other than my physical therapy exercises, the trainer doesn't want me working out with the team at all for another month.
>
> PARENT: How else might you show up for the team, even if it's not as a player?
>
> ATHLETE: There is nothing for me to do except sit on the bench. Honestly, it feels like a waste of my time.
>
> PARENT: How might your presence support the other players?
>
> ATHLETE: I don't know. Sure, they like me cheering them on, but after a while, it gets old. And I'm not sure there's any value of that during practice.

PARENT: I'm sure it does get old. Especially when you wish you were playing. It must be hard.

ATHLETE: So what are you getting at?

PARENT: Imagine the coaches were talking about you and the role you are playing on the team now as a former starter. What would you want them saying about you?

ATHLETE: I guess I'd want them to say I was still a leader. But I can't do that when I'm not playing or practicing.

PARENT: Think back to last year when you were in the NCAA tournament and things were stressful. How might a leader on the sidelines have helped you during this time?

ATHLETE: Well, we could have used help keeping our focus. There were times we would get angry with one another and having someone help us stay level-headed would have been nice.

PARENT: What else?

ATHLETE: Maybe just having someone there to pick up the balls, bring over water. The team managers do all that, but sometimes it's nice to have a player do that.

PARENT: How might that impact the way the team sees you?

ATHLETE: I think they'd see me as more invested. It would probably help when I return to playing as well.

PARENT: If you were to rank yourself on a scale of 1 to 10 for how well you've been supporting your team while recovering, how would you rank yourself?

ATHLETE: Honestly, probably a 5 or a 6.

PARENT: What would it take to get to an 8 or 9?

ATHLETE: I don't know.

PARENT: What would it look like if you asked Coach what he thinks you could be doing now to 'lead' from the sidelines?

ATHLETE: He could probably give me some specific duties to help. Maybe I could do something for the freshmen, or help with the second team. That would be better than just sitting and cheering from the bench. Maybe I'll ask him.

Showing up for the team, especially when sidelined with an injury, can be difficult, and yet it is a common occurrence. Research suggests that elite athletes have an injury prevalence rate three to five times higher than the general population.[10] When injured, they may lose connection to the team. The physical, psychological, and social loss, even if only temporary, can be significant, and make showing up for the team when injured even more challenging.

For many athletes, knowing how to be present for the team while injured is helpful. Strategies might include assisting in practice, organizing the locker room, supporting the trainer, or helping younger players acclimate to the team. It might require an athlete to 'manage-up' and initiate a conversation with the coaching staff to see where they can contribute while recovering.

We conclude this chapter by featuring New Zealand's infamous men's national rugby team, the All Blacks. They are a great example of servant leadership team orientation. Known for their 75 percent winning record over the last 100 years, the All Blacks have been the subject of numerous studies to understand the leadership and culture that contribute to such success.[11] In his book *Legacy: What the All Blacks Can Teach Us about the Business of Life*, James Kerr describes the 15 All Blacks principles.[12] One of the team's mottos, "sweeping the sheds," conveys the value of humility and reinforces the idea that no one is too successful to clean up the locker room or do any task related to team performance. Another motto, "better people make better All Blacks," highlights the importance of character over talent. The motto "plant trees that you'll never see," captures the ultimate act of selflessness required of members to preserve the legacy of the team.

The All Blacks culture explicitly values the skill of listening and is built upon each player taking ownership for the team so that there is shared responsibility, accountability, and trust. Sacrifice also stands as a core value in the context of current and future devotion to the team. The awareness of the needs of others, both now and in the future, is a driving force for this club, where leadership is delivered by all team members, not just the captains.

As with the All Blacks, athletes who learn to show up with a servant leadership mentality and commit to the success of the team add significant value both on and off the field. In the final chapter, we will talk about how you as a parent can show up for the team in ways that support your athlete and the team's overall success.

Conversation Questions

To wrap up, we offer these questions for you to ask your athlete when the types of situations described in this Pillar arise.

- *What value do you bring to your team both on and off the field?*

- *What does supporting your teammates' success look like to you? What value can you gain from doing this?*

- *In five years, how do you hope the coaches and fellow players will speak about your contributions to this team?*

- *How can you dig deep, even when you're disappointed, and show up for your team?*

- *If you were to give advice to an incoming player about how they could best support the team, what would it be?*

Questions for Your Reflection

How might your child contribute to a positive emotional culture even in difficult situations?

_____

_____

What value (both athletic and personal) does your child believe they bring to the team or organization?

_____

_____

What value (both athletic and personal) do you believe your child brings to the team or organization?

_____

_____

Where might your child have opportunities to lead and positively influence the team?

_____

_____

How You Can Show Up to Support Both the Athletes and Team

Throughout this book, you have read about conversation strategies to help your athlete navigate the world of elite athletics. These conversations can support the development of intrinsic motivation, resilience, a growth orientation, and ultimately the ownership of an athlete's experience. Each of these areas of development can help your athlete perform at increasingly competitive levels and thrive in the world beyond sports. However, navigating these intentional conversations can be difficult, if not impossible, when you become emotionally triggered and upset.

It's been said that when you have a child, a part of your heart forever lives outside your body. It hurts to see your child frustrated, angry, and disappointed. The painful emotions you might feel when you watch your athlete burn out, make poor choices, or seemingly throw away all the work she's done, can be overwhelming. It can also be gut-wrenching to witness your child realize that she may not have the skills to play at the next level and struggle to come to terms with these limitations. At these turning point moments, it is completely natural to have strong emotional reactions that spur you to protect, judge, discipline, rant, rescue, instill guilt, or pity your child in ways that aren't helpful to her.

Just as with your child, when your emotions are triggered, a fight, flight, or freeze response is activated that can impede the region of your brain responsible for solving problems, reasoning, creating understanding, holding multiple perspectives, and making decisions. When these moments occur, consider the acronym TIME as a guide to lower your emotional intensity so that you can best serve your child.

T: Take several belly breaths and pause.

I: Identify the impact and outcome you want to create.

M: Manage your emotions to create an outcome rather than react to the situation.

E: Engage your athlete with the long game in mind.

You might not always like the way you handle situations. Sometimes conversations go badly and exchanges with your athlete can feel disastrous. You might find yourself yelling instead of remaining calm or talking negatively about the coach and later regretting it. When this happens, it's helpful to go back to your child, apologize, and work to repair what went wrong. Often, an apology can bring you closer to your athlete, and modeling recovery from missteps with grace and humility provides invaluable role-modeling for your child. As the writer Robert Fulghum once said, "Don't worry that children never listen to you; worry that they are always watching you."

It is worth noting several specific situations that can trigger intense emotional reactions. One triggering situation may occur if your athlete decides she no longer wants to play but you still feel heavily invested in her life as an athlete. As we acknowledged earlier, your role in your child's athletic career has been instrumental, and you have most likely made great sacrifices to help her get to where she is today.

Sue has worked with many collegiate athletes who continue to play when their heart is no longer in the game just because they don't want to disappoint their parents or fail to meet their parents' expectations. As you can imagine, this situation is not a recipe for success. It is one of the reasons we have written at length about helping athletes develop autonomy and intrinsic motivation.

Navigating the crossroads of leaving a sport after years of time, physical and financial investment can be extremely difficult for both the parent and the athlete. If you encounter this experience, know that your own feelings of significant grief and disappointment are only natural. Having someone with whom you can process your emotions can be hugely beneficial so that you can support your child in her decision-making process.

Another common challenge parents face arises when they are co-parenting and have different perspectives on their child's athletic journey. As we mentioned in Pillar 4: Show Up Ready to Communicate and Manage Your Relationships, triangulation between parent, coach, and athlete can put undue stress on an athlete. The same holds true when triangulation happens between an athlete and two parents; mixed messages and competing advice can create confusion and stress.

If you co-parent, the more you both can do to present a united front, the less potential stress you create for your child. Steps you can take together might include agreements on when to approach conversations, how to talk to her about her goals and processes, and supportive behaviors you want to demonstrate during games and competitions. There is no doubt that coming to such agreements can be extremely difficult, and it may require you to find your own trusted support system to process your differences. However, determining strategies for you and your co-parent to serve your child's well-being as the central goal will make all the difference in your athlete's experience.

It is also helpful to consider how you show up and contribute to the parent culture of a team. Coaches are the first to acknowledge that this culture can easily enhance or undo a team's hard work. In this way, the parent culture plays a pivotal role in a team's success. Yet, it can be hard to manage. Parent culture is influenced by the relationships between parents and coaching staff, between parents and other players, and among fellow parents. When interacting with others involved in your child's athletic community, demonstrating a positive attitude, modeling healthy conversations, maintaining appropriate boundaries of support without interference, and keeping the long game perspective will contribute to a healthy and productive environment for your athlete.

What gets in the way?

Parenting an elite athlete can be complicated. You may find yourself walking through your own emotional landmines alongside the complex emotions of your athlete and of the team culture. Perhaps the greatest interference we see is when parents don't pause to process and acknowledge their own feelings of frustration or disappointment separately from those of their athletes'. A helpful metaphor is to think about the airplane guidelines for an emergency situation: When the oxygen masks drop, place your mask over your own nose and mouth before securing someone else's mask. Processing and regulating your own emotions first will allow you to be present and agile in ways that best support your athlete.

One specific behavior that raises concern for many coaches and directly impacts both the individual and the collective team is how parents talk to their athletes immediately before and after a competition. It is natural to want to share final words of advice before your child steps into competition. However, when parents impart their wisdom right before an athlete competes, it can interfere with her focus and the coach's preparation process.

The same is true after an event. If parents offer their perspective immediately following a competition, it can cloud the athlete's experience. Young adult athletes need to learn to go inside and self-evaluate. This process is critical for developing an internal feedback loop as discussed in Pillar 8: Show Up Ready to Receive and Process Feedback. In addition, most coaches have specific strategies to help athletes process their collective performance after a competitive event, before parents offer their own perspectives.

Before competition, a great rule of thumb is to simply tell your athlete good luck, you love her, and you look forward to watching her compete. After the game, tell her that you enjoyed being there to support her and her team. Keep it simple and short. You will be creating an enormous gift of time and space for your athlete's learning and development.

It's also important for parents to be mindful of sideline conversations that can significantly impact the team culture. Conversations among parents questioning a coach's decision or a player's performance can take a negative turn very quickly. If you find yourself part of a conversation that feels ripe with drama, you can support your athlete and her team by simply disengaging. Consider politely excusing yourself and moving away or rerouting a downward spiraling discussion by asking an unrelated question.

It is easy to get caught up in team drama. As parents of athletes ourselves, we have both been guilty of this trap. To resist, imagine either your athlete or the coach is sitting with you and hearing the conversation. Or ask yourself, "A year from now, what would I like to say about how I handled this moment?" Knowing that you play a role in your athlete's overall experience can provide the motivation to disengage from negative situations.

Again, if you are experiencing a challenging dynamic on the team that has you feeling personally frustrated, ask yourself if this challenge is yours or your child's. If it is your child's, think about how you can support her to take initiative and manage the situation on her own. If the challenge is yours, however, how can you handle the situation in a direct way to bring about a positive outcome and avoid involving others or creating team drama? How you respond in such situations directly impacts the team's culture and that in turn impacts your child's experience.

By managing your interactions with other parents, coaches, and players, you can create a parent-team culture that mirrors the best athletic experience you wish for your athlete.

Finally, talking negatively about coaches or other players directly with your athlete may cause unintended stress for her. There are times your child might need to rant to you, and you may think you are empathizing if you participate directly in her venting. Keep in mind, however, that you may be inadvertently putting your child in a difficult situation if you do this. Ranting with her can fuel her frustrations, and even worse, it can ultimately create divided loyalties. As your child climbs the competitive ranks, her coach will play a significant role in her development and her future. If she thinks that you dislike a coach with whom she has to sustain a working, professional relationship, it can create anxiety for her. She might even feel that she is expected to take sides.

To get out of this trap, you can simply listen when your child needs to vent. Acknowledge that she is frustrated but do not contribute to her commentary. Playing a listening role does not mean that you have to like or approve of the decisions your child's coach makes. It does mean that you can support your child working through her frustration more effectively if you remain neutral and help her identify what she can do to influence the situation.

A similar problem may arise when you express judgment and dissatisfaction with the other players. If you are inclined to share your own frustration over another player's mistake or poor performance, your child may fear your negative reaction if she should make a similar mistake. Sadly, we have worked with anxious athletes who worry about their parents' judgment of both their own and others' performance. So, when your athlete is venting about a teammate's mistake, your role is to provide a listening ear and remain as neutral as possible.

How can you help your athlete by being mindful of how you show up?

As we have mentioned throughout this book, the role you play in your child's success is pivotal. Athletes who have a positive relationship with a parent or guardian have an emotional bond in which the adult is available, sensitive to distress signals from the child, and responsive when called upon to provide comfort.[1] A growing body of research confirms that athletes who have this kind of bond with a parent or guardian are more likely to thrive and experience high levels of performance and well-being. Your challenge is to show up in a positive way that nurtures your relationship and helps your athlete develop the autonomy to flourish.

Let's end by revisiting some of the comments shared in the opening chapter from athletes about their parents and the ways they showed up.

What do you wish your parents knew about your life as a college athlete?

- Parents won't understand the coaches' decisions and what goes on with the team completely and that's okay. Parents should be there to support you, but not to be involved in what goes on.

- Yelling and being mad at me for my mistakes isn't going to make me any better.

What do your parents do that is helpful to you as an athlete?

- One thing they do that is helpful is not stepping in. They just let me do what I need to and learn for myself.
- They are always there to vent to as an outsider and they give me space.

What do your parents do that is not helpful to you as an athlete?

- My parents have been amazing, but sometimes they need to just listen when I tell them things and not act. Sometimes I am just thinking out loud or venting, and that doesn't require them to do anything after.
- They compare me to other people or to teammates.

What could your parents do to better support you as a collegiate athlete?

- Help me when I ask, but stay reserved when I want to deal with something myself.
- I need time before I talk about games or results. I am someone who wants to talk through those things, but sometimes I want to wait a bit to talk about them so I can individually process how I feel first.

These athletes want both support and autonomy. They want to be heard but they also want to navigate challenges on their own. They want their parents to be involved in their athletic experience and community, but they want space and opportunity to learn about themselves, their sport, and the interpersonal dynamics of working with others. It's a tall order to be sure. Parents are asked to provide empathy and attention to their child's changing needs.

There is great opportunity to think intentionally about how you want to show up as a parent. You might reflect on the relationship you are cultivating with your child now and in the future. There are great rewards and great challenges in parenting promising elite athletes. Nothing is more exciting than watching your athlete excel and succeed. At the same time, watching your child struggle through obstacles can be equally painful and frustrating.

As a parent, you are uniquely positioned to help your athlete balance the short and long game of sports. By supporting your child's autonomy in the present, you are helping her to become the best athlete she can be. And in teaching her to integrate the lessons of sport, you are helping her to learn to become a fulfilled adult.

You are truly giving her the gift of a lifetime.

Questions for Your Reflection

What are your hopes for your child in athletics and in life?

_____

_____

How are these hopes aligned?

_____

_____

In 10 years, what do you hope your child says about your relationship during her athletic career?

_____

_____

What is one thing you could start doing today to nurture the parent-athlete relationship you wish to create?

_____

_____

Acknowledgments

Many people supported and helped us to write this book. Without each of them we would not have had the information or fortitude to complete this project. First and foremost, we would like to thank our families: Cole, Maggie, Max, Shawn, Molly, and Finn. Each of them offered encouragement, patience and humor when we needed it, all of whom give our lives meaning and purpose beyond the work we do and love. Second, we thank our parents for inspiring us to be lifelong learners and teachers.

We would also like to thank the many coaches who took time to meet with us and review our work. In particular we would like to thank Jamie Franks without whom this project would never have happened. He was a source of inspiration and provided the opportunity that helped us see there was a need for this handbook. We are grateful that he shared his experience as a coach and gave us our first opportunity to work with the parents of a team of elite athletes. Other coaches who shared invaluable insights and stories include: Chris Cartlidge, Lynn and Mike Coutts, Logan Davis, Ron Grahame, Melissa Kutcher, Maureen Roben, and Scott Yates. Thank you all for sharing your expertise and time with us.

We shamelessly asked several friends who had elite athlete children to read drafts and give us feedback. Thank you to Dr. Lisa Billings, Wendy Brandes, Sean Breeze, Alessandra Herman, Rob and Julie Hill, Cole Mehlman, Liz Palmquist, Paulette Sanchez, Ladan Schlichting, and Anna Sommers for your feedback and careful reading. Four colleagues, Jessica Bartely, Psy.D., Emily Clark, Psy.D., Tom Golightly Ph.D., and Sheila Ohlsson Walker, Ph.D., also generously offered their expertise and time to review our work and give us feedback.

We received excellent support from two research assistants, Sean Mapoles and William King. Both were prompt and thorough in their work to find and assess relevant research and to review the book. Sean continued to be a helpful resource throughout the book writing process.

Special thanks to the following professionals for their guidance: Hilary Morland for her exceptional copy-editing work; Sue Collier for her expertise and keeping us on track; Erika Osherwow for her proofreading, and Shaun Tyrance, Ph.D. for sharing his publishing experience. And thank you to Dan Cronin, LISAC, Brian F. Shaw, Ph.D., and M. David Lewis, M.D., for the introduction to this field.

Last but not least, we would like to thank all of the athletes and parents of elite athletes we have worked with over the years who shared their stories with us. We appreciate their thoughtful, honest insights into their parent-child relationships. Because our work requires confidentiality, we can not name them and have disguised their identities in the stories and data we shared. Each of you has contributed in some way to this book, and we are enormously grateful.

ABOUT THE AUTHORS

Maureen Breeze is the principal at Cultivage, an executive coaching and corporate training company, and the co-founder of Retreat Reinvent Recharge, an international organization that supports women's career advancement. She is an adjunct professor at the University of Denver's Center for Professional Development teaching business leaders some of the strategies discussed in this book. Prior to this work, Maureen served as the Senior V.P. for LifeBound, an education consulting firm, where she developed academic coaching programs to help universities and colleges support students' success. She presented her methodology at conferences throughout the U.S. and in Switzerland, Germany, Spain, China, and Mexico. Maureen's first career was as a dancer and choreographer, and she continues to coach dancers launching their professional careers. She received her undergraduate degree in International Management and Mathematics from Claremont McKenna College, and studied dance performance & choreography in graduate school at U.C.L.A.

Suzanne B. Schimmel, Ph.D. received her undergraduate degree in psychology from Yale University and her Ph.D. in clinical psychology from Boston University. She has a private practice in Denver, Colorado, working with athletes at the collegiate, Olympic, and professional levels. Within that domain, Sue focuses on mental health issues, retirement from sport and addictions treatment. She has been consulting to a Division I men's sports team since 2017. More recently, she helped create programming for the United States Olympic & Paralympic Committee mental health team for the transition out of sport. Sue has produced informational videos on relationship issues for the health and wellness committee of the National Hockey League Players Association, and has provided therapy for athletes from the National Hockey League and Major League Soccer for over 15 years.

REFERENCES

How You Can Help Your Athlete Show Up for Optimal Performance

1. Cote, J. (1999). The influence of the family in the development of talent in sport. *The Sport Psychologist, 113, 395-417.*

2. Cote, J., Baker, J., & Abernathey, B. (2007). Practice and play in the development of sport expertise. In R. Eklund & G. Tenenbaum (Eds.), *Handbook of Sport Psychology* (3rd ed., pp. 184-202). Wiley.

3. Lowe, K., Dorsch, T. E., Kaye, M. P., Arnett, J. J., Lyons, L., Faherty, A. N., & Menendez, L. (2018). Parental involvement among collegiate student-athletes: An analysis across NCAA divisions. *Journal of Intercollegiate Sport, 11*(2), 242-268. https://doi.org/10.1123/jis.2018-0028

4. Arnett, J.J. (2015). *Emerging adulthood: The winding road from the late teens through the twenties* (2nd ed.). Oxford University Press.

5. Arnett, J.J. (2000). Emerging adulthood: A theory of development from the late teens through the twenties. *American Psychologist, 55,* 469-480. https://doi.org/10.1037/0003-066X.55.5.469

6. Dorsch, T. E., Lowe, K., Dotterer, A. M., Lyons, L, & Barker, A. (2016). Stakeholders' perceptions of parent involvement in young adults' intercollegiate athletic careers: Policy, education, and desired outcomes. *Journal of Issues in Intercollegiate Athletics, 9,* 124-141.

7. Kaye, M. P., Lowe, K., & Dorsch, T. E. (2019). Dyadic examination of parental support, basic need satisfaction, and student-athlete development during emerging adulthood. *Journal of Family Issues, 40(2),* 240-263.

8. Parietti, M. L., Pastore, D.L., & Sutherland, S. (2017). Parental involvement in the lives of intercollegiate athletes: Views from student-athletes and academic advisors for athletics. *Journal of Amateur Sport, 3(3),* 106-134.

9. Arain, M., Haque, M., Johal, L., Mathur, P., Nel, W., Rais, A., Sandhu, R., & Sharma, S. (2013). Maturation of the adolescent brain. *Neuropsychiatric disease and treatment, 9,* 449-461. https://doi.org/10.2147/NDT.S39776

10. Borelli, J. L., Burkhart, M. L., Rasmussen, H. F., Smiley, P. A., & Hellemann, G. (2018). Children's and mothers' cardiovascular reactivity to a standardized laboratory stressor: Unique relations with maternal anxiety and overcontrol. *Emotion, 18*(3), 369-385. https://doi.org/10.1037/emo0000320

11. Amorose, A. J., Anderson-Butcher, D., Newman, T. J., Fraina, M., & Iachini, A. (2016). High school athletes' self-determined motivation: The independent and interactive effects of coach, father, and mother autonomy support. *Psychology of Sport and Exercise, 26,* 1-8. https://www.sciencedirect.com/science/article/abs/pii/S146902921630054

12. Kegelaers, J. (2019). *A coach-centered exploration of resilience development in talented and elite athletes.* Universiteit Brussell, Vubpress.

13. Morelli, S. A., Torre,& J. B., Eisenberger, N. I. (2014). The neural bases of feeling understood and not understood. *Social Cognitive & Affective Neuroscience,* 9(12), 1890-6. https://doi.org/10.1093/scan/nst191

Pillar 1

1. Dweck, C. (2007). *Mindset: The New Psychology of Success.* Ballantine Books.

2. Burns, D. D. (1999). *Feeling Good: The New Mood Therapy.* William Morrow.

Pillar 2

1. Murray, R. (2012, June 12). Hope Solo: Olympians train hard but party harder. *New York Daily News.* https://www.nydailynews.com/sports/olympics-2012/hope-solo-olympians-train-hard-party-harder-article-1.1113139

2. Seligman, M. (2006). *Learned Optimism: How to Change Your Mind and Your Life*. Vintage.

3. Van Yperen, N.W., Blaga, M., & Postmes, T. (2014). A Meta-analysis of self-reported achievements goals and nonself-report performance across three achievement domains (work, sports, and education). PLoS ONE, 9(4), e93594.

4. Williams, J., & Krane, V. (2021). *Applied Sport Psychology: Personal Growth to Peak Performance*. McGraw-Hill Education.

5. Lizmore, M. R., Dunn, J. G., Causgrove Dunn, J., & Hill, A. P. (2019). Perfectionism and performance following failure in a competitive golf-putting task. *Psychology of Sport and Exercise*, *45*, 101582. https://doi.org/10.1016/j.psychsport.2019.101582

6. Curran, T. (2018). Parental conditional regard and the development of perfectionism in adolescent athletes: The mediating role of competence contingent self-worth. *Sport, Exercise, and Performance Psychology, 7*(3), 284-296. https://doi.org/10.1037/spy0000126

7. Hamid, A. A., Pettibone, J. R., Mabrouk, O. S., Hetrick, V. L., Schmidt, R., Vander Weele, C. M., Kennedy, R. T., Aragona, B. J., & Berke, J. D. (2015). Mesolimbic dopamine signals the value of work. *Nature Neuroscience*, *19*(1), 117-126. https://doi.org/10.1038/nn.4173

8. Kaku, M. (2021). *Physics of the Future: How Science Will Shape Human Destiny and Our Daily Lives by the Year 2100*. Anchor Books.

9. *Megan Rapinoe: Twice Removed, But Never Gone—U.S. Soccer.* (2009). Https://Web.Archive.Org/Web/20130621222423/Http://Www.Ussoccer.Com/News/Other/2009/03/Megan-Rapinoe-Twice-Removed-but-Never-Gone.Aspx. Retrieved April 28, 2022.

10. *Megan Rapinoe: Twice Removed, But Never Gone–U.S. Soccer.* (2009). https://web.archive.org/web/20130621222423/http://www.ussoccer.com/news/other/2009/03/megan-rapinoe-twice-removed-but-never-gone.aspx   Retrieved April 28, 2022.

Pillar 3

1. Sternberg, R. J. (1999). The theory of successful intelligence. *Review of General Psychology, 3*(4), 292–316. https://doi.org/10.1037/1089-2680.3.4.292

2. Zemke, R., Raines, C., & Filipczak, B. (2013). *Generations at Work: Managing the Clash of Boomers, Gen Xers, and Gen Yers in the Workplace* (Second ed.). AMACOM.

3. Gaudreau, P., Morinville, A., Gareau, A., Verner-Filion, J., Green-Demers, I., & Franche, V. (2016). Autonomy support from parents and coaches: Synergistic or compensatory effects on sport-related outcomes of adolescent-athletes? *Psychology of Sport and Exercise, 25*, 89–99. https://doi.org/10.1016/j.psychsport.2016.04.006

Pillar 4

1. Darby, J. (2021, October 18). *How journaling can help you stay positive*. Olympics.com. https://olympics.com/athlete365/well-being/how-journaling-can-help-you-stay-positive/

2. Civico, A. (2017, August). *Master the 7 steps to conflict transformation*. Mediate.com. https://www.mediate.com/articles/CivicoATransformation.cfm

3. Zemke, R., Raines, C., & Filipczak, B. (2013). *Generations at Work: Managing the Clash of Boomers, Gen Xers, and Gen Yers in the Workplace* (Second ed.). AMACOM.

4. Sherman, L. E., Michikyan, M., & Greenfield, P. M. (2013). The effects of text, audio, video, and in-person communication on bonding between friends. *Cyberpsychology: Journal of Psychosocial Research on Cyberspace, 7*(2). https://doi.org/10.5817/cp2013-2-3

5. Johnson, W. (Host). (2020, September 29). Zaza Pachulia: The game of disruption (No. 183) [Audio podcast episode]. In *Disrupt yourself podcast with Whitney Johnson.* https://whitneyjohnson.com/zaza-pachulia

Pillar 5

1. Deci, E. L., & Ryan, R. M. (2013). *Intrinsic motivation and self-determination in human behavior.* Springer Publishing.

2. Calvo, T. G., Cervelló, E., Jiménez, R., Iglesias, D., & Murcia, J. A. M. (2010). Using self-determination theory to explain sport persistence and dropout in adolescent athletes. *The Spanish Journal of Psychology, 13*(2), 677–684. https://doi.org/10.1017/s1138741600002341

3. Walton, G. M., & Cohen, G. L. (2007). A question of belonging: Race, social fit, and achievement. *Journal of Personality and Social Psychology, 92*(1), 82–96. https://doi.org/10.1037/0022-3514.92.1.82

4. Bubbs, M. (2019). *The new science of athletic performance that is revolutionizing sports.* Chelsea Green Publishing.

5. Overskeid G. (2021). Can Damasio's somatic marker hypothesis explain more than its originator will admit? *Frontiers in psychology, 11*, 607310. https://doi.org/10.3389/fpsyg.2020.607310

6. David, S. (2018, January). *The gift and power of emotional courage.* [Video]. TED Conferences. https://www.ted.com/talks/susan_david_the_gift_and_power_of_emotional_courage

7. Goleman, D. (2015). *Focus: The hidden driver of excellence.* HarperCollins.

Pillar 6

1. Goleman, D. (2020). *Emotional intelligence: 25th anniversary edition.* Bloomsbury Publishing.

2. Tan, S. Y., & Yip, A. (2018). Hans Selye (1907-1982): Founder of the stress theory. *Singapore medical journal, 59*(4), 170-171. https://doi.org/10.11622/smedj.2018043

3. Brackett, M. (2020). *Permission to feel*. Celadon Books.

4. Lange, A.M., A.W. Kruglanski, & Higgins E., (2011). *Handbook of theories of social psychology*. Sage Publications.

Pillar 7

1. Ellis, B. J. & Boyce, W. T. (2008). Biological sensitivity to context. *Current Directions in Psychological Science, 17*(3), 183-187. https://doi.org/10.1111/j.1467-8721.2008.00571.x

2. Seligman, M. (2021, April). Building Resilience. *Harvard Business Review Magazine*. https://hbr.org/2011/04/building-resilience

3. Sinclair, R., & Cheung, J.H (2017). The right stuff: Employee characteristics that promote resilience. In M.F. Crane (Ed.), *Managing for Resilience: A Practical Guide for Employee Wellbeing and Organizational Performance, (pp. 13-30)*. Routledge.

4. Mischel, Walter. (2014). The marshmallow test: why self-control is the engine of success. Little, Brown & Company.

5. Zemke, R., Raines, C., & Filipczak, B. (2013). *Generations at Work: Managing the Clash of Boomers, Gen Xers, and Gen Yers in the Workplace* (Second ed.). AMACOM.

6. Bubbs, M. (2019). *Peak: The New Science of Athletic Performance That is Revolutionizing Sports* (1st ed.). Chelsea Green Publishing.

Pillar 8

1. Ericsson, K. A., & Pool, R. (2017). *Peak: Secrets from the New Science of Expertise.* Mariner Books.

2. Scott, K. (2019). *Radical Candor.* St. Martin's Press.

3. Slack Team. (2019, June 5). Serena Williams's stroke of genius for overall success: The tennis star serves up thoughts on

teamwork, feedback and focus. *Slack Blog.* https://slack.com/blog/collaboration/serena-williams-stroke-of-genius-for-overall-success

Pillar 9

1. Harley, L. (2019, September 12). *The road to greater performance: How team sports can benefit from emotional contagion.* BelievePerform—The UK's Leading Sports Psychology Website. https://believeperform.com/the-road-to-greater-performance-how-teams-sports-can-benefit-from-emotional-contagion

2. Gordon, J., & West, D. (2019, March 24). *THE COFFEE BEAN by: Jon Gordon and Damon West.* [Video]. YouTube. https://www.youtube.com/watch?v=TWszGs3v6UO&ab_channel=TheDamonWestChannel

3. Goncalves, Joana (2009, February 4). Relationship between Team Sports Cohesion and Success. Group Dynamics. https://groupdynamics.webnode.com/news/team-sports-cohesion-and-success-what-is-the-link/

4. McEwan, D. (2020). The effects of perceived teamwork on emergent states and satisfaction with performance among team sport athletes. *Sport, Exercise, and Performance Psychology, 9*(1), 1-15. https://doi.org/10.1037/spy0000166

5. Rieke, M., Hammermeister, J., & Chase, M. (2008). Servant Leadership in Sport: A New Paradigm for Effective Coach Behavior. *International Journal of Sports Science & Coaching, 3*(2), 227-239. https://doi.org/10.1260/174795408785100635

6. Allas, T., & Schaninger, B. (2021, May 7). *The boss factor: Making the world a better place through workplace relationships.* McKinsey & Company. https://www.mckinsey.com/business-functions/people-and-organizational-performance/our-insights/the-boss-factor-making-the-world-a-better-place-through-workplace-relationships

7. Smith, M.K. (2013, March 2). *Bruce W. Tuckman – forming, storming norming and performing in groups.* Infed.Org: education, community-building and change. https://infed.org/mobi/bruce-w-tuckman-forming-storming-norming-and-performing-in-groups/

8. Civico, A. (2021, June 8). *Conflict Coaching: The 7 Steps to Transform Any Conflict* [Video]. WBECS. https://www.wbecs.com/wbecs2018/presenter/aldo-civico/

9. Leading Effectively Staff. (2021, August 23). *Improve Talent Development Conversations With SBI Feedback Model.* Center for Creative Leadership. https://www.ccl.org/articles/leading-effectively-articles/sbi-feedback-model-a-quick-win-to-improve-talent-conversations-development/

10. Lemoyne, J., Poulin, C., Richer, N., & Bussières, A. (2017). Analyzing injuries among university-level athletes: prevalence, patterns and risk factors. *The Journal of the Canadian Chiropractic Association*, *61*(2), 88-95.

11. Johnson, T., Martin, A. J., Palmer, F. R., Watson, G., & Ramsey, P. (2012). Collective Leadership: A Case Study of the All Blacks. *Asia Pacific Management and Business Application*, *1*(1), 53-67. https://doi.org/10.21776/ub.apmba.2012.001.01.4

12. Kerr, J. (2013). *Legacy: What the All Blacks can teach us about the business of life.* New York: Little, Brown and Company.

How You Can Show Up to Support Both the Athletes and Team

1. Davis, L., Brown, D. J., Arnold, R., & Gustafson, H. (2021). Thriving through relationships in sport: The role of the parent–athlete and coach–athlete attachment relationship. *Frontiers in Psychology*, *12*. https://doi.org/10.3389/fpsyg.2021.694599

INDEX

Motivational Interviewing (MI), 19

National Collegiate Athletic Association (NCAA)
  research on parental involvement, 13
  research on parental support, 69

Niebuhr, Reinhold, 41

norming stage of team development, 133

opportunity spotting, 50

optimism, 105, 109

overgeneralizing, 27

oxygen mask metaphor, 147

oxytocin, 69-70

Pachulia, Zaza, 72-73, 81

parent culture, 146

parental involvement
  college athletes' views on, 15-17, 149-150
  co-parenting challenges, 146
  emotionally intense reactions, managing, 144-147
  expectations of, 12-13
  giving feedback, 120-123, 135-137, 147
  importance of, 13

intervention, harms of, 54-56, 65-66
  positive, 13
  pre- and post-competition conversations, 147
  protective responses, harms of, 106-107
  reflection questions, 23, 152
  as supporting independence, 14
  in team drama, 147-149

passive language, 56-57

passivity, resisting, 51

perfectionism, 40

performance anxiety, 38-39, 94

performing stage of team development, 133-134

Permission to Feel (Brackett), 93

personalizing, 27

Pillars of Success, 18. See also specific Pillars

POWER acronym for attributes of resilience, 104-106

practical intelligence, 52

practice, smart, 115

predicting the future, 27

proactivity and resourcefulness (Pillar 3)
  about, 50-54

conversation strategies, 56-60
  dialogue example, 58-60
  obstacles to, 54-56
  parental reflection questions, 62
  questions to ask, 61

problems
  anticipating, 50-51
  solving, 32, 46, 51-52, 55-56, 57

process orientation, 37-38

professional mindset (Pillar 5)
  attributes of, 76-81
  conversation strategies, 83-86
  dialogue example, 84-86
  obstacles to, 81-83
  parental reflection questions, 88
  questions to ask, 87

protective responses, parental, 106-107

purpose, sense of, 104

questions, asking open-ended, 19-20, 96-97

Radical Candor (Scott), 122

Rapinoe, Megan, 46

relationship management. see